D1597764

tying
terrestrials
for super fishing

tools, tips & tricks
for tying everything from grasshoppers to inchworms

C. BOYD PFEIFFER

The Countryman Press
Woodstock, Vermont

Copyright © 2008 by C. Boyd Pfeiffer

First edition

Library of Congress Cataloging-in-Publication Data has been applied for

ISBN 978-0-88150-763-8

Book design and composition by Carol J. Jessop, Black Trout Design

Cover and interior photographs by the author

Published by The Countryman Press, P.O. Box 748, Woodstock, VT 05091

Distributed by W. W. Norton & Company, Inc., 500 Fifth Ave., New York, NY 10110

Printed in China

10 9 8 7 6 5 4 3 2 1

CONTENTS

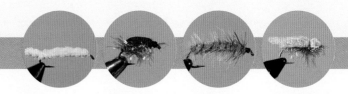

Illustrates basic fly tying tools and materials, including substitutes for other standard tying materials: Tools include vises, lights, threads, sealers, bobbins and bodkins, hackle pliers, and foam punches. Materials covered include yarns, tinsels, chenilles, stranded body material, hackle, foam, wing materials, body hair, and leg materials for tying excellent terrestrials of all types.

Covers the basics of tying, including tying down, tying off, handmade whip finishes, use of cyanoacrylate glues, positioning materials, adding foam in myriad ways, using felt tip pens, fabric paints, and furling materials to make extended bodies.

Documents ant imitations distilled down to basic designs, with variations of ants and termites including foam ants, McMurray styles, fur and thread underwater ants, Chernobyl ants, egg-casing ant patterns and more. Termites—basically imitations of long-bodied ants in white—are also covered extensively.

Teaches basic beetles and Vince Marinaro's jassid, including many ways to tie imitations of the insects that are the mainstay

CONTENTS

terrestrials taken by trout, panfish, and some bass. The use of coffee beans, foam, deer hair, McMurray-style bodies, yarn, and back materials are all included, along with ways to make beetles in all varieties; long or short, thin or bulky, and in all colors and sizes.

(by furling techniques) large earthworms, red manure worms, and similar worms that are the fly fisherman's equivalent of the standard live angleworm.

A NOTE TO THE READER

All instructions in this book assume right-handed tiers who work with the jaws of the fly-tying vise pointed to the right and who handle thread bobbins with their right hands. If you are left-handed, then instructions and hand-use directions will have to be reversed. The same applies to the photos; all show a right-handed tier's perspective. Also, many photos have been taken with larger-than-normal materials and thread for the sake of clarity.

Please note that there are references to using lead wire and lead dumbbell eyes. In some areas, lead is prohibited; these materials will therefore have to be eliminated or replaced with non-lead substitutes.

DEDICATION

To Brenda

ACKNOWLEDGMENTS

Both close friends and strangers can teach us a lot about fishing if we only listen and learn. All of my friends have been more helpful than they could ever realize in all of our fishing ventures. They have also helped with thoughts and ideas at get-togethers and fishing trips, on the phone, and during casual conversations. Naturally, this help involves all types of fishing and tying—including that of terrestrials and terrestrial fishing. To all my friends—you know who you are—my heartfelt thanks.

Strangers have also helped with tips, techniques of terrestrial fishing, and ideas on tying; no matter where we have met, my thanks to them also. Thanks also go to Rainy Riding, of Rainy's Flies & Supplies and Bill Skilton of Bill Skilton's USA-Flies. Both helped with ideas and materials for this book, and that is appreciated. Both have top-quality materials for tying terrestrials and other flies.

My particular thanks to my publishers at Countryman Press, editors Kermit Hummel and Jennifer Thompson, and associates. They allowed me extra time to complete the text and photos after a knee operation. Somehow, I find pain a distracting element when trying to write, thus this additional time during a long recovery helped tremendously.

Finally, my thanks to my wife Brenda, who forgives me the time that I take to crawl into my "cave" (as she calls it—I think of it as an office), to work on and complete various writing projects.

I could never make it as a commercial tier. I tried it once during high school, and it did not take. I just did not like the repetitiveness of tying the same thing, ad infinitum (as I would think of it). Even today, whether tying a particular pattern or trying to develop a new design of fly, I somehow get to thinking about changes, simplifications, adjustments, modifications in tying steps, etc. Before I know it, or by the fourth or fifth fly, my original thought of a good standard pattern has morphed into something else.

In some ways, this is fine. It means that my imagination or desire for something new, something different, something simpler, keeps me going in an effort to come up with the obviously impossible—but still sought after—perfect fly. At other times, it is less than desirable, as when I am trying to fill—or refill—a fly box with a specific pattern that is a must for some future fishing trip. I like tying, and particularly like tying terrestrials, but often end up more often with a box that shows the evolution of a design or pattern rather than neatly regimented rows of identical flies. This changing of designs mid-stream or mid-hook is a disease that seems to be particularly virulent with terrestrial tying. Often, these simple bugs are tied with only various pieces of foam, in a variety of colors and sizes designed to resemble a wide gamut of land critters that now and again fall into the drink; they just lend themselves to easy morphing, changing, and modifying.

Many of the flies in this book are a result of this wayward thinking and tying and are meant to be representative of the types of flies designed today, and in the recent past, to imitate the various terrestrials involved in all types of fishing. It is not—and is not intended to be—a definitive listing of every terrestrial fly ever designed. First, that would be too exhausting an undertaking; including all terrestrial patterns would be impossible. Second, the repetitiveness of such a listing would not be to the advantage of any tier or fly fisherman. There are unique styles to the designs of each tier and to every region, and variations of basic flies based on very specific terrestrial species. To try to cover them all would be repetitive and would result in a book being obsolete by the time it came off the press.

There are other books on terrestrials, terrestrial fishing and terrestrial history, many of which are listed in the bibliography. In addition, many—maybe most—fly tying books have sections on terrestrials. Some of these sections are small, some are large, but any terrestrial inclusion speaks of the importance of these flies. The same applies to general freshwater fly-fishing books, many of which include sections on techniques and methods of fishing terrestrials.

There is one book that I would strongly recommend, even though it is not an exclusively terrestrial book: *My Fly Patterns, Materials and Techniques* by Bill Skilton. It provides a good look at the tying innovation and skills of this tier, who in my opinion is highly talented yet underrated by the tying public. He sells neat materials and ties highly effective, innovative flies. I am a big fan of his—his tying skills and patterns. His book can be ordered on-line from **www.billskilton.com**, where his unique materials can also be ordered; or write to Bill Skilton's USA-Flies, P. O. Box 60, Boiling Springs, PA 17007-0064.

Another good source for materials is Rainy Riding's company, Rainy's Flies & Supplies, 690 North 100 East, Logan, UT 84321. A good source for McMurray-style bodies, for ants, beetles, and bees, is Rod Yerger, P.O. Box 294, Lawrence, PA 15055.

chapter

TOOLS AND MATERIALS

Tools for tying terrestrials are no different from basic tying tools. Beginning fly tiers usually have most tools required for tying great terrestrials. If anything, fewer tools are required; for instance, the need for a gallows tool, usually used for making posts for parachute flies, is minimal, as is any need for dubbing teasers or spinners for dubbing loops. While for some terrestrials a dubbed body is beneficial, it is not necessary if you want to go simple. Here is what is needed and why:

Vise. Get a good, but basic, vise. Ones with large jaws, as are found on vises for tying saltwater flies, as well as those with minute jaws required for tying the minutia of sizes 18 and smaller, simply are not necessary. Though there are some tiny (smaller than size 16) terrestrials such as ants and beetles, these are the exception and only a few are ever needed. Most terrestrials are tied on size 16 and larger hooks—up to about size 2.

Vises with collet tightening or the lever-style jaws both work fine. The collet type works by means of an arm operating a cam that pulls the two jaws back against a collet to tighten the jaws on the hook. The lever type uses a thumb screw to separate the jaw lever bars at one end. A fixed center fulcrum forces the other end (the working end) of the jaws to tighten and hold the hook. Some vises, such as the HMH vises, have removable/replaceable jaws for tying different sizes of flies so that one can choose jaws based on the type of fly being tied.

I like a clamp-style vise at home, since it can be adjusted vertically and clamps securely to my bench. For travel, I use a pedestal vise. The advantage of the clamp vise is that it holds securely and is adjustable in height. The advantage of a pedestal vise is that it can be taken anywhere and be used on any flat surface. This is particularly good for tables that are too thick for the clamp or where a clamp might mar a table edge or surface. The disadvantage of a pedestal vise is that the base makes it heavier than a clamp-style vise.

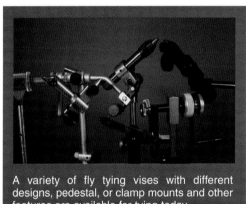

A variety of fly tying vises with different designs, pedestal, or clamp mounts and other features are available for tying today.

For a tier planning a lot of tying and turning of materials on the hook shank, consider a rotary vise such as a Renzetti, Norlander, or one of the many brands (Abel, Dyna-King, Griffin, and others) that have models with this option. Rotaries (or those that allow turning if not a true rotary) are helpful in that they allow inspection of the other side (back of the tying side) of any fly. Otherwise, they are not necessary.

Light. Good lighting is critical for precise tying. Special fly tying lights are available, including those that have daylight bulbs to replicate sunlight (about 5500 degrees Kelvin). These are available in freestanding or vise-clamping styles. Small, simple halogen lights are good for most fly tying operations. You can also get along nicely with a small student's desk lamp taking a standard bulb (usually 60-watt). A good alternative today is one of the 15-watt twisted-bulb screw-in fluorescents. They save money, are as bright as an old-style

Get at least two pairs of scissors—one with fine short blades for delicate cutting and one with longer, coarser blades for cutting heavy materials. Serrated blades—or one serrated, one smooth—make it easier to cut materials such as synthetics that would otherwise slip.

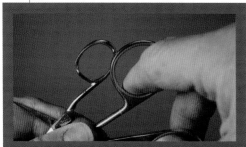

Be sure to buy scissors with large finger holes that are comfortable to use—do not get women's cuticle scissors from the drug store.

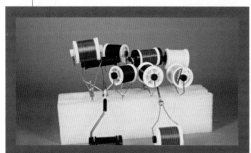

Several bobbins make it easy to store and use several different tying threads of different sizes and/or colors. For best results, purchase only those with ceramic tips to prevent thread wear and fraying.

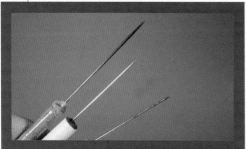

You can buy or make bodkins, which are basically needles mounted in short handles. Bodkins are used for depositing head cement on the heads of flies or for freeing materials that you have inadvertently bound down with thread.

60-watt, and generate less heat. All of these are relatively inexpensive. Just be sure that any light chosen provides good lighting of the fly and sits high enough over the vise to allow good clearance over the hook shank for all tying operations.

Scissors. Owning several good fly tying scissors is critical. Very fine pairs, such as those used for tying tiny dry flies, are unnecessary, but one small pair along with one larger pair for cutting coarse materials is the minimum. Coarse, or heavier, materials are used often in tying terrestrials; buy fly tying scissors (not drug-store cuticle or toiletry scissors) that have large finger holes, and those with one serrated edge are best to prevent materials from slipping as you cut them.

Bobbin. Tying without thread bobbins is possible, but tying is easier with bobbins. If possible, get a half-dozen so that constantly switching spools and rethreading—each time thread sizes, colors, or flies change—is kept to a minimum. Get only those with ceramic rings at the tip end to prevent thread wear. Those with a long tube are best, since they allow more "reach," as when tying big flies and bugs, or when tying at the rear of a fly, which is often necessary with some terrestrials. Bobbins are also good for working with fine stranded materials other than thread. Use them for fine chenille, floss, yarn, lead/non-lead wire, colored wire, tinsel, etc. Save old thread spools so that you can fill them with these materials—which are not usually available spooled.

Bodkin. A bodkin (a needle on a handle) is a must-have for pulling out hackle accidentally bound down with thread, applying a tiny drop of head cement, or fraying out body material, etc. They are available commercially, or can be made by inserting a large needle, eye first, into a four-inch length of wood dowel (after first, drilling a tiny hole) and gluing it in. Keep several different sizes handy for different tying purposes.

Hackle pliers. Hackle pliers are a must-have also, to wrap hackle around a hook shank, and useful for holding and wrapping other materials. Several styles are available—the spring-type English style, the wire or rod-type English style and rotary styles. The latter have small gripping jaws attached to a universal hinged joint and shaft/handle. They allow gripping the material to wrap around a hook shank without repositioning the pliers (to prevent twisting) as required with other styles.

The above tools are the basics and probably are all that are needed for most simple flies, but more can be added, as follows:

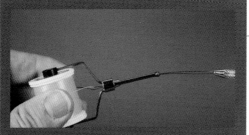

Here the bobbin threader is being pulled out of the bobbin shaft to pull the thread with it. The thread was run through the large opening in the wire bobbin threader to make this possible.

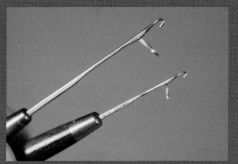

Latch hook tools are available from several manufacturers with these from Rainy Riding available in two sizes as shown. They are ideal for making a knot in feathers such as turkey to make the bent legs used in tying hoppers.

Comb. Use a small cosmetic, eyelash or moustache comb for combing out underfur from animal skins. Use the underfur for dubbing or discard it when removing it from guard hair to make wings and throats.

Latch-hook tool. These are available from most shops and catalogs, and are useful for tying overhand knots in rubber legs or feather bundles to make bent hopper legs. Several sizes are available and instructions are included.

Foam punches. These come in two types—round pipe-like for punching out cylinders, and shaped punches for making shaped foam bodies. Both types are available from most fly shops and catalogs. Use the round type on thick foam (i.e., flip-flops on sale at end of summer season) to punch out cylindrical bodies for terrestrials, employing a thin dowel to push the punched body out of the sharpened tubing.

    The shaped body punches, of formed, sharpened steel, punch out a body shape from thin foam for tying down on a hook. They have one open end to lever out the foam bodies. Many shapes are available and they usually come in sets of three.

Dubbing teaser. Dubbing teasers are rough, to fray out and "fuzz" materials to create a shaggy/buggy look. Many commercial types are available—or make one from the hook side of hook-and-loop fastener (Velcro), with a small patch of the material glued to a popsicle stick. Another possibility is using a toothbrush, ground down on the sides of the brush end to make it narrow, with the bristles clipped short.

Half-hitch tool. These small tapered tools with a hole in one end are ideal for making half-hitches to secure various tying steps or finish a wrap on a fly head. They are best for the intermediary steps in tying; a whip finisher is best for finishing a fly.

    Use a half-hitch tool by first looping the thread around the tool, then placing its hole over the hook eye and pulling the

Foam punches are available in round cylinders for punching out cylinders of foam or like these that are shaped for making bodies out of sheet foam. Most of these come in a set as shown and are available in different body shapes for making all kinds of foam bodies for terrestrials.

Example of using a sheet foam body punch and punching out a body—in this case a black cricket body.

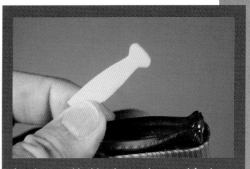

As above, with this shape also used for hoppers as shown with this yellow sheet foam body produced.

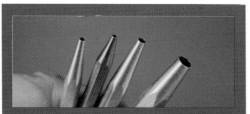

Half-hitch tools are ideal for making locking wraps on a fly to hold materials securely and to prevent slipping.

Using a half-hitch tool requires making a loop of the thread around the tapered end of the tool, and then positioning the hollow end of the tool over the hook eye to slide the thread into the hook shank. Because hook sizes and eyes vary so widely, several sizes of half-hitch tools are available for this.

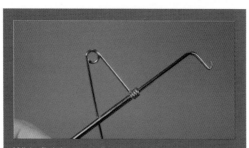

Whip finishes can be done with your fingers or with a whip finisher tool as shown here.

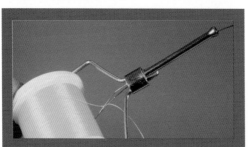

Bobbin threaders come in several styles, but all are designed to fit into the sleeve of a bobbin and to grab in some way the thread to pull it out through the sleeve of the bobbin. Some are like latch hook tools and others—like this one—are like needle threaders used by seamstresses.

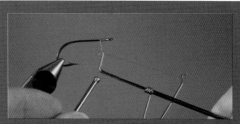

You can use your fingers to make a whip finish or use tools such as this whip finisher. Follow the directions to make sure that you are wrapping the thread around the hook correctly. This is the beginning step in which the thread is gathered in a loop for wrapping around the hook shank.

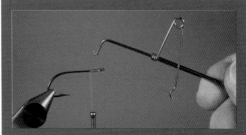

Step two in using a whip finisher is to wrap the thread around the hook shank as shown here.

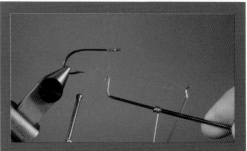

The final step after making several turns of thread is to release the loop from the tool and pull the thread tight against the hook shank.

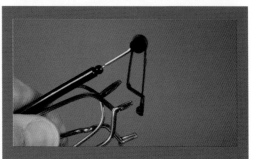

Hackle pliers are available in several different styles, including rotating hackle pliers. These prevent twisting materials as you wrap.

thread to slide the loop off of the tapered tool and onto the hook shank or the head of the fly. If using these for intermediary steps in tying, the tool must have a deep hole to allow sliding it back on the hook shank to the proper position for the half-hitch.

Whip finisher. Use only fingers to make a whip finish in any fly (I do) or use one of the available tools for this purpose. These are available in two styles, with the Matarelli making it possible to make a whip finish on any part of the fly, while other brands allow making a whip finish only at the head of the fly. With just fingers, any number of whip finish wraps on any part of the fly can be made at any time.

Tool rack. Tool holders and organizers made of wood, foam or plastic include a variety of round and square holes of different sizes to hold everything from bodkins to head cement bottles, from scissors to whip finishers. They are useful to keep tools handy, neatly organized and not scattered over the bench.

Bobbin threader. These simple tools, mostly thin wire or mono loops, are ideal for easily threading a bobbin; insert the loop of mono or wire through the bobbin tube, push the thread from the spool through the loop, and simply pull out the thread with the loop. One can be made by sharply folding some 12-pound monofilament (or thin braided fishing wire) and then knotting the two ends (mono) to make a thin loop. Fold a self-stick label across the knotted ends so that you do not lose it on your tying bench; or glue the ends into a hole drilled into the end of a short dowel to make it look more tool-like—this is particularly good when using wire.

Bobbin cleaner. Bobbins ultimately become clogged with wax from threads. Bobbin cleaners are thin rods, or thick, short lengths of mono, for cleaning wax out of a bobbin tube. One can be made from a single short length of thick mono from any lawn trimmer. As with the bobbin threader, adding a folded self-stick label, or a four-inch wood dowel for a handle, prevents loss.

Material dispensers. These come in a wide range of types and styles, depending upon the materials and the manufacturer. They include: plastic compartment boxes with holes in the bottom (through which stored dubbing can be pulled from the turned over box); small bottles, bins and round plastic containers for beads; spool containers (i.e. Spirit River) for stranded materials such as chenille and yarn; pill-like compartment-containers for hooks and beads; racks and tubes for flash strands, etc. They are not necessary but they are very handy. They make any fly tying quicker, easier, and more organized.

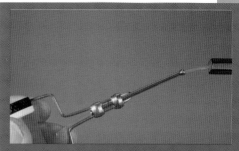

Bobbins will in time build up wax in the sleeve (shaft) which must be removed for smooth use of the bobbin and to get the thread through the shaft. For this, you can use a commercial bobbin cleaner or a similar thick length of mono or weed-whacker type of mono to fit into the shaft and clean out any wax.

Many types of storage boxes and systems are available for fly tying tools and materials. This multi-compartment box holds small items, in this case beads for weighting flies. These can also be used for holding hooks, foam bodies, hopper legs, or other small parts used for tying terrestrials.

Racks for hanging stranded flash materials are available to make these instantly available and readily visible. Flash is often used in making terrestrials by using a few strands for the wings of ants, beetles, bees and such.

Just remember that the basics of fly tying are simple. A sturdy vise, a good light source, a bobbin or two to hold thread, two pairs of scissors (one fine/delicate, one sturdy/coarse), hackle pliers, and a bodkin are necessary. Other tools can be added as desired, or when needed for particular patterns or tying steps.

MATERIALS

Hooks. Hooks for most terrestrial tying range from about size 16 to 2, but can also be larger or smaller as required for the fishing. Ed Engle, in his book *Tying Small Flies,* writes of tying ants down to size 24, while for cicadas and some Western late fall grasshoppers a hook size 1 or larger might be needed.

Many hooks are available not only in regular but also longer and shorter shank lengths. These are indicated by an "X" system, with 1X short indicating a hook that has a shank length of the next smaller hook size and 1X long indicating a hook with a shank length of the next larger size hook. Hooks are available from about 3X short to 10X long.

A similar "X" system is used to describe hooks that are made of finer or stouter wire than standard. A hook 2X finer for dry fly fishing would have a wire of a hook two sizes smaller, while a 2X stout hook would be made with wire for a hook two sizes larger. Sometimes the very small hooks are made with stouter than normal wire to prevent hook bending from the fine but stronger leader tippets that are available today.

The basics of fly hook design revolve around the bend of the hook. Some are completely symmetrical (Perfect bend) while others have a squared-off bend (Sneck). Some have an almost round bend (Aberdeen), while others have a sharper kink at the lower part of the bend (Limerick, O'Shaughnessy, Sproat). Some few hooks have special shank configurations for salmon fishing (Dublin, Wilson, York), and others have very curved specialty shanks for making shrimp, scud, and nymph patterns. All of these can be used for tying terrestrials, but the simplest basic hooks are often the best. They are also easiest to get, least expensive to buy, and simplest for most tying.

Eyes on hooks are also important. As a general rule, I like straight eyes, but hooks with turned up and turned down eyes are available. Note that if you use a Turle knot or George Harvey dry fly knot to tie your tippet to a fly, you must use a hook with a turned-up or turned-down eye. This allows the leader to pass through the hook eye with the knot in back on the fly head when pulled tight. This assures that the fly sits right and performs correctly.

Most hooks needed for terrestrials are straight-shank, with a straight or down-turned eye, and in regular length up through 4X long, depending upon the style of fly being tied and the terrestrial being imitated. For an ant, use a regular length hook, while for an inchworm a 2X long hook is best, and for a caterpillar a 4X hook shank allows for the most effective imitation.

Size, however, is not the only factor; always consider other hook styles. Examples would be scud or shrimp hooks, or the 37160 Mustad that comes in a variety of sizes and is great for tying a caterpillar that is curling up as opposed to one that is as straight as a cased fly rod. For small bugs and patterns for bluegills and other panfish, consider a 6X or 8X long shank. This allows having a length of hook shank in front of the tie by which to pry the hook out of the small mouths of these fish. (More on this in Chapter 2.) For foam-, balsa- or cork-bodied terrestrials, consider some of the small size hump- or kink-shank hooks designed for bass bugs, poppers, and sliders. These reduce the possibility of the body twisting on the hook. They are best with a long shank such as the Mustad 33903 for both easier striking and easier unhooking of the fish once landed.

All of this affects how you tie and what you tie, and can also affect which materials—and the number or amount of materials—that you use to tie terrestrials. For example, if you can use a heavy wire hook that helps sink a panfish bumblebee imitation, it may eliminate the need for added weight such as a small dumb bell eye, cone head, wrap, wire or similar weight additions. Similarly, a light-wire hook for a hackle style jassid dry might lessen the need for more dubbing or hackle to help float the fly.

For those interested in more details on hooks, and for a ready reference as to most of the hooks available, check out *Hooks for the Fly,* by William E. Schmidt, Stackpole Books, Mechanicsburg, PA, 119 pages.

Thread. Thread is essential to fly tying, notwithstanding the fact that many tiers—and especially tiers of terrestrials—seem to get heavily into glue and goo these days. As with hooks, there is a multitude of thread choice available from many fine manufacturers of good nylon threads in many styles, colors, and sizes, from 3/0 to 15/0. Although you do need a variety of thread sizes, depending on whether you are tying a size 4 grasshopper or a minute size 24 ant, you can get by with only a few basic colors in these. My general choices of thread colors are as follows:

Thread in almost any color and in many sizes is available from several main manufacturers including Gudebrod, Uni, Danville, etc.

Black—Ants, beetles, jassids, bees, wasps, hornets, crickets, spiders, roaches, ladybugs, flies, caterpillars, cicadas

White—Termites, cicadas, caterpillars, butterflies

Red—Red ants, cinnamon ants, worms, ladybugs, red manure worms

Yellow—Inchworms, caterpillars, leaf hoppers, katydids, butterflies,

Light green—Inchworms, caterpillars, leaf hoppers, froghoppers, treehoppers, katydids, butterflies, early Spring grasshoppers.

Brown or dark tan—Fall grasshoppers, butterflies, spiders

A good general rule is to match the color of the thread to the principal colors, materials, and components of the fly being tied.

Thread sealers. Thread sealer, also called head cement, is used to coat, penetrate, and seal the thread-wrapped head of a fly to protect it, keep the whip finish from unraveling, and to sometimes provide a base on which you can paint eyes. These sealers are available in environmental-friendly brands (Loon Outdoors) as well as petroleum and chemically based solvent-style sealers. Many fly tiers use clear Sally Hansen Hard as Nails fingernail polish, since it is easy to get and easy to use, with an application brush in each bottle. Taper or cut the brush to make application easy on small flies, or use a bodkin for this purpose.

See Chapter 2—Simple Tying Steps and Special Tricks, for more details of sealer application.

Hackle. Hackle is widely available through any fly shop or a number of mail order catalogs. Hackle is a feather or feathers typically from the neck or cape of a bird. Chicken is widely used, but hackle is also available and used from grouse, wood duck, pheasant, and other wild game.

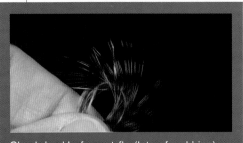

Feathers such as these examples are used for hackle, wings, and other parts of flies in terrestrial tying.

Check hackle for wet fly (lots of webbing) or dry fly (little webbing) by bending the vane and holding it up to see the webbing between and on the individual fibers as is shown here.

To check for the type of hackle, hold a single feather up to the light to see the amount of webbing between the individual fibers. Dry fly hackle has very little webbing—since any webbing soaks up moisture and causes a fly to sink rapidly or to not float well. Use this type for surface ant, jassid, termite, and beetle patterns; it helps to float the fly if there is no other flotation involved in the pattern.

Wet fly hackle has a lot of webby fibers central to the main vane of the feather. As a result of this water absorbent web, such hackles are ideal for wet flies or flies that sink. Use wet fly hackle for underwater flies such as ants, bumblebees, termites, beetles, etc.

A popular type of fly today are soft hackle flies that have longer than normal (at least longer than in the past) hackle fibers to make for a very buggy fly with a lot of action and movement in the water. These hackle are also good in terrestrial tying for patterns such as bumblebees, beetles, underwater ants, etc.

You can buy hackle by the neck or by the half neck, as well as by packets of individualized fibers and long "saddle" hackles of a given size that are good for a multitude of flies. Chicken hackle comes in a wide range of natural and dyed colors.

Feathers. Hackle is feather, but not all feather is hackle, at least by fly tying definitions. Among the mix popular for terrestrials are marabou, chickabou, turkey, peacock herl, ostrich herl, emu, duck quills and wings, guinea, etc. Marabou and chickabou have great action in the water, and can be used for some underwater patterns. Mottled turkey is great folded over a body to make a fall grasshopper wing. Peacock, ostrich, and emu herls are good for bodies and heads on some terrestrial patterns.

Yarn. Yarn is a good body material for a number of terrestrial flies. Both synthetic and natural material yarns are available, with synthetics usually the least expensive and the best. Multiple thicknesses and colors are available, including hard polished yarn and soft fuzzy types, variegated colors, and various textures. It is good for bodies of ants, beetles, termites, grasshoppers, crickets, caterpillars, worms, etc.

Yarn is a basic body material for lots of underwater terrestrials. It is available in a wide variety and range of colors, sizes, texture, and materials in fly shops and craft and art supply stores.

A type of yarn newly available in craft and sewing stores has a lot of fringe, almost like a shortened body fur; some styles are dense, others are straggly looking, but all have potential in tying flies including terrestrials. I like them particularly for making a wrap or using the fringe to simulate legs on a beetle or ant.

Chenille. Chenille comes in both tight twist chenilles, such as Ultra Chenille and Vernille, or the "standard" stuff that is fine for most purposes. You can also get chenille that is variegated, along with the cactus chenilles (ice chenille, Estaz) that are a sparkly plastic-like product. In addition, chenille comes in many sizes. Vernille or Ultra Chenille is best for making small worms such as red manure worms, while standard chenilles are fine for making bumblebee patterns and tying up bodies of beetles and flies. The ice or cactus chenilles are ideal for making larger worms for bass fishing, as well as legs for small beetles.

Chenille is also available in many colors and sizes from fly tying and craft stores. It is popular for tying a lot of terrestrials of all types.

Floss. Floss is made of very fine stranded material, either silk or synthetic, and is used to make shiny, smooth bodies on flies. It is often used when tying terrestrials in order to make smooth-bodied underwater red, black and cinnamon ants, or to make beetle bodies. As with other materials, it is available in many sizes and colors.

Synthetic dubbing. Working with standard dubbing is time consuming and not necessary for terrestrials patterns. It requires cutting, mixing furs and/or synthetics, then waxing thread (or forming a working thread loop to twist in the dubbing) prior to wrap-

Synthetic dubbing or stranded dubbing material such as EZ-Dub from Gudebrod makes it easy to tie a lot of different terrestrial patterns.

ping around the hook shank. Fortunately for terrestrial tiers, you can also get stranded dubbing materials such as Gudebrod E-Z Dub, Rainy's No-Dub, E-Zee Bug, mohair, and others. These all have a ragged, buggy appearance in very life-like colors, yet are easy to tie onto a hook, as you would yarn. The shaggy looking craft yarns mentioned above are also ideal for these purposes.

Stranded flash materials. By adding a tiny bit of stranded flash materials (such as Flashabou, Krystal Flash, Super G Flash and others) to a wing of a fly imitation, beetle or grasshopper, you add fish-attracting flash. Sometimes this is good for wings, splayed out or wrapped over the body of a terrestrial. The secret is to use only a tiny bit—not the large, long bundles often added to streamer fly wings.

Wire, tinsels, and such. Metal and plastic (often Mylar) tinsels are available in many colors and sizes for making shiny bodies. Often this is best used when tying beetles, either topwater or underwater. Wire is becoming increasingly important in fly tying, with most of these being enameled non-tarnish styles that are available in many sizes and colors.

Lead (non-lead) wire. Wire for weight (added by wrapping around the hook shank or laying parallel and then tying down) is available in lead and non-lead products in many sizes. In some areas, the use of lead is prohibited for fishing (this may also include brass, which has trace amounts of lead). In these situations, you must use non-lead products in your flies. A half-dozen sizes of lead or non-lead wire are available. Since most terrestrials are going to be free floating or swimming in the current or drifting in still water, lead is used infrequently in terrestrial tying.

Furs. Furs are taking a backseat to the many synthetics available today. Some furs are still irreplaceable for some aspects of fly tying. Rabbit fur is popular for its action. Calf tail is useful for short wings and parachute posts on some terrestrial flies.

Deer and body fur. Deer hair (along with elk, moose, caribou, antelope) is used in terrestrial flies by tying down and then folding over the hook shank to make a beetle body —as in the Crowe beetle and some ant patterns. For this, you want fine hair, such as antelope or coastal deer hair. You can spin and stack deer and other hair to make a terrestrial body, but it is far more work than necessary. Use heavier hair such as moose for legs and antennae. Deer hair is also popular and useful for making wings for grasshoppers, and when dyed black, for crickets. It is used also when making bullethead (Thunder Creek style) hoppers.

Rubber leg materials of rubber, silicone and Lumaflex are available in solid and mottled colors as the samples shown here. They are ideal for larger terrestrial legs on hoppers, spiders, beetles cicadas and crickets.

Beads and cone heads. Beads and small cone heads are ideal for adding weight to underwater terrestrial patterns. Go easy on this, since terrestrials fall into the water but usually do not sink—or sink deeply—before being eaten; they just float or drift along on or within the surface, or slightly underwater, as would any struggling or downed and drowned insect.

Use the smallest possible bead or cone and stick to light metals, avoiding heavy tungsten. Many shapes and colors are available, and all may be added, though only to barbless hooks or those in which the barb has been bent down. A Perfect Bend hook is best for this, to allow sliding the bead around from the point to just in back of the eye. Use plastic beads if you want no appreciable weight but only color.

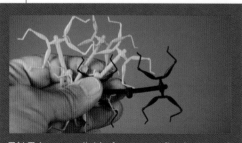

T.N.T. legs, available from most fly shops and catalog houses make it easy to make the rear hopper legs on hopper and cricket patterns. They come in pairs, twelve to a pack.

Rubber/silicone legs. Thread a few rubber or silicone legs through the foam, cork, or balsa body of a terrestrial bug and you automatically add some action and make a bug better. You can tie these into the side of any terrestrial pattern for more action. Several materials (rubber, silicone) are available, in several thicknesses and in solid colors, in variegated, banded, and other patterns. In addition, molded hopper legs are available in several colors. These make great substitutes for the overhand-knotted feather legs for the same purpose.

Foam. Foam cylinders, formed foam bodies and sheet foam are ideal for terrestrials. Cricket and hopper bodies in several sizes and shapes are available from all fly shops. All types of foam come in a dozen or more colors and in many sizes. The foam bodies and cylinders are available in sizes ranging from about ¹⁄₁₆ inch to about 1 inch. Sheet foam is available in sizes from about 0.5 mm to about 6 mm (¼ inch) thick. This is great stuff for shaping into beetles, ants, crickets, hopper bodies, etc.

Pre-shaped and formed bodies for making trout terrestrials are also available. Rainy Riding, for example, has shaped foam bodies for general terrestrials (Gorilla Foam Bodies) in four or five-segment types and in nine colors including two-tone laminated bodies. Also available, from Rainy Riding, Bill Skilton, and others, are banded foam cylinders—for making bees and wasps—along with foam-cylinder ant bodies that have a bright colored end for visibility. Other manufacturers make half-oblong foam bodies for making crickets, which are also good for making beetles and ants.

Cork/balsa bodies. Cork and occasionally balsa are available in pre-shaped body forms, along with standard bottle corks. To make simple bugs without the necessity of sanding, shaping, cutting, polishing and sawing, use pre-shaped bullet foam, cork and balsa bodies.

Paints. Paints add another dimension and a step or three to making any bug, since you might have to first fill pits (i.e. in cork), then coat the bug body with a primer, then add two coats of the finish. If you do decide to use paints, get all-purpose enamels or the specialty paints such as the "soft" paints from Rainy Riding for painting foam bugs. Normal hard paints chips off such bugs when the foam is compressed.

Foam in cylinders, shaped bodies and sheets is available for making all kinds of floating terrestrials. Many colors, densities and sizes are available.

Foam strike indicators to self stick or be glued to terrestrials make it easy to see small terrestrials as they float downstream. These are from Bill Skilton's USA-Flies and consist of dots or rectangles in many colors.

chapter

There are a number of ways in which to save time, and yet still make very effective terrestrial flies. The following are some general tips that later in this book will be explained in detail when tying specific patterns:

Tying on with glue. Some patterns do not require a lengthy or extensive wrap on the hook. An example would be the McMurray ant. To get a secure wrap with only a few turns of thread, coat the hook shank with head cement or fingernail polish and with the sealer still wet, tie on the thread. Clip the excess thread and continue tying. The glue or sealer binds the thread to the hook shank for a permanent bond.

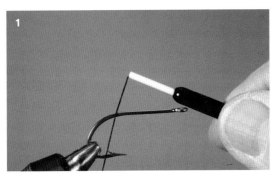

Begin tying on by holding the thread with the bobbin against the hook shank as shown here, then wrapping around the hook shank.

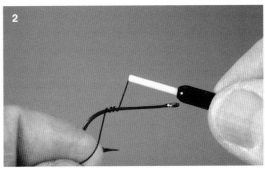

Step two in tying on is to make the wraps around the hook shank as shown.

To secure the thread to the hook, hold the thread in place, then cross over the wraps of thread with the thread held in the bobbin as shown. This can be aided by wrapping over a wet coating of head cement to both wrap and glue the thread in place.

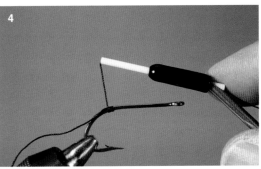

Finish by making a few wraps of the thread around and over the previous wraps to secure the thread. Then clip the tag end of the thread, unless leaving a long tag end for segmenting a foam body or other tying tasks.

Tying off with fingers. Learn to tie off flies with a whip finish, using your fingers. You can do this easily by first learning with heavy thread on just a bare hook, then progressing to large flies, and finally to all flies.

The secret is to use your fingers just as you would a whip finisher, only using your right hand to wrap the thread around the hook shank while holding the standing end of the thread with your left hand. Finish by using a bodkin to support the thread loop to prevent knots as you pull the whip finish tight. You can use just two wraps, or many wraps/loops, depending upon which is needed on a particular fly.

To make a whip finish with your fingers, hold the bobbin with your left hand and then place your index and middle finger on the thread as shown.

Next, roll your hand to form a loop in the thread as shown.

Continue by turning your hand while holding the loop in place so that you can use your fingers to wrap the loop around the hook shank.

Here, the thread loop is being wrapped around the hook shank. Wrap several times for best results and a tight wrap.

When finished, remove one finger from the loop as shown and then hold the loop with a bodkin so that it will not tangle or knot.

Here the loop is being held with a bodkin and the end of thread pulled tight as the bodkin prevents the loop from tangling or knotting.

Using thumb nail to position whip finish. Position a whip finish by using your left thumb nail while holding the thread and wrapping the loops with your right-hand fingers. Do this to correctly position the final wraps so that the whip finish is smooth and positioned exactly where you want it on the head of the fly. This still allows for holding the standing thread with fingers of your left hand.

Untwist thread to flatten it for thin ant waists. Hang a bobbin from a hook and the tied thread gradually untwists. Use this technique to flatten the thread wrap where needed, as when wrapping up the hook shank after tying in an abdomen on an ant pattern or wrapping around the waist area where you want the thinnest possible wrap for a slim waist on the fly.

Make long body for termites; wasps. There are several ways to make long bodies for some terrestrial patterns, such as required when tying a termite, hornet, or wasp pattern. One way is to use a long shank hook so that you have a longer hook shank on which to wrap the body material or otherwise make the body to simulate the shape of these insects.

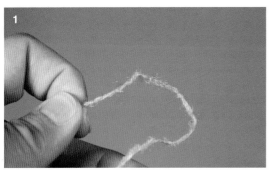

To furl yarn, chenille, or other stranded materials, hold one end stationary and then roll the other end in your fingers, twisting it to make it fold on itself when released. This can also be done by securing one end of the material on the hook shank and then twisting the other end.

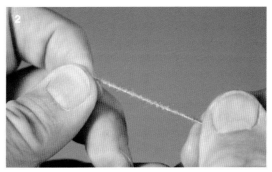

Here the furled yarn is twisted, but still held straight prior to folding to make the doubled furled body. Make sure that the twist is in the same direction as the twist used to manufacture the material.

Here the furled and twisted yarn has been folded on itself to make a doubled, twisted (furled) body.

This furled-yarn body material can be tied down on a hook to tie an extended-body terrestrial.

Another way is to make a furled body. For this, you can use yarn, or stranded dubbing materials such as E-Z Dub, or chenille. There are two ways to make and use a furled body. One is to first twist the material, then hold together the two ends of the length needed while the material furls on itself; with thread already in place on the hook shank, tie down these two ends so that the twisted and furled body extends in back of the hook shank. The result is an extended body or abdomen.

The other way to do this is to tie in the length of furling material on the hook shank, then use your fingers to twist the end so that it folds on itself and furls as you tie this loose end down on the hook shank. In doing either of these methods, make sure that you twist in the same direction in which the material was manufactured in order to prevent it from coming unraveled. This is particularly true of chenille and ice chenille.

Preventing foam body rotation. One problem with tying foam beetles is that most instructions suggest tying down at the rear of the hook shank, adding other materials, and then folding the foam over the hook to tie down at the front to complete the foam body. The problem is that this tie-down at one spot often allows the foam body to rotate while tying or fishing. This might not seem bad, but could be a disaster if the body rotates to 90 degrees or more to impede the hook gap. It could result in a missed fish or prevent solid hooking of a strike.

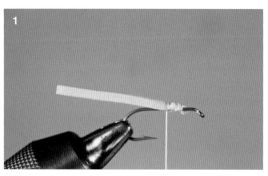

To prevent foam from twisting on a hook, first tie down at the middle of the hook, as shown, before progressing to the rear of the hook as follows.

Continue the thread wrap down the hook as shown to secure the foam to the hook and to prevent twisting prior to folding over the foam to make a body.

After making the above steps, then wrapping the thread forward to a tie-down point, you can fold the foam over the hook shank and tie down. Tying down in the middle assures that the foam will not twist.

To prevent this, first tie in the thread at the middle of the hook shank, tie down the fold-over foam material, and wrap thread to the rear of the hook shank. Then, wrap forward before folding over the foam and tying down the head or thorax of the terrestrial at the front of the fly. This step of wrapping the foam on the middle of the fly and wrapping towards the rear stabilizes the foam to prevent it from rotating on the hook shank while fishing. Finish the fly with a wrap of legs, and any back or wing materials.

An alternative way of doing this is to tie down the foam at the rear of the fly, making sure that you have a long enough piece of foam to extend forward over the hook shank. Wrap the thread over the hook shank and foam to the front, then fold over the foam and tie down as above to finish the fly. The result of the completed tie is the same.

Note that in doing either of these, you must plan for an added length of foam for this additional wrap to stabilize the foam.

Use teflon tape for white bodies. One tip originally developed for making crane fly larva flies is to use white Teflon tape for white bodies. You can use this same plumber's tape for making white bodies of termites, wrapping on a long shank hook, and building it up to make some bulk to the long abdomen of these insects. If you wish to protect the tape body, use thread or fine nylon monofilament to rib or segment the body. Note that white thread does not show on a white body, while black or colored thread makes distinct segments in the body.

Taper foam to fold over for beetles. Easy foam beetle bodies may be made with flat or sheet foam, cut to size and shape, then tapered and tied in at the rear of the hook shank. Tie down the point or tapered end of the shaped beetle body at the rear of the hook shank, or follow the previous instructions on stabilizing the foam body. Then wrap the thread forward up the shank. Fold the foam over the hook shank and tie down with thread to make the beetle abdomen or body. Realize that in addition to cutting foam with scissors or a blade, you can use the foam body punches listed under "Tools."

An easy way to secure foam is to taper one end for wrapping onto the hook shank so that the foam will not spin after being tied down and folded over.

Adjusting beetle and terrestrial length, shape. By using regular hooks or long shank hooks and adjusting the length and shape of the foam, you can tie any style of beetle, from short and round to long and slim. Legs of deer hair, hackle, rubber leg material, or wraps of Estaz may be added to any beetle to make a variety of patterns and looks.

You can also use readily available pre-shaped cricket bodies for making beetles, since these usually have a tapered end. This allows the foam to be tied down easily, then folded over and secured with the thread that has been advanced on the hook shank.

Using phosphorescent materials. Phosphorescent materials are used for the tail or rear of firefly imitations. This allows the rear of the terrestrial to glow, just as would the cold light of a firefly or lightning bug struggling in the surface film of water. To make this phosphorescent material work, expose the fly to the sun during daylight fishing. Since these often work best during evening or night fishing when fireflies are out, also carry a small flashlight for this purpose. An alternative is to use the smallest and least expensive photo electronic flash to "pop" the fly for instant "charging" of the phosphorescent material.

Punch pocket in plastic for spider abdomen. A neat way to make spiders is to make a "bag" of a square of clear plastic, into which you insert dubbing material or short-clipped yarn to make spider body. It is like a miniature version of packing a lunch into a square bandana for a picnic, or making a steelhead bait bag with mesh material. One way to make this easier and more realistic is to use a rounded prod to push into the square of plastic, making a pocket. Use the eraser end of a pencil—rounded—and push this into the plastic, or pull the plastic over that end of the pencil. Do not tear the plastic. Other round items also work well for this step. This makes tying down the plastic easier and creates a realistic, smooth-skinned spider abdomen appearance when filled with dubbing.

Seal foam first before cutting to save time. On some terrestrials (beetles, ants, bees) you might want to seal the foam with head cement or other sealers to simulate the shiny body or carapace of the natural. To do this and save time, seal the entire sheet of foam before cutting the foam into strips and pieces. That way, the foam is sealed when you tie the fly, reducing time and also preventing the possibility of getting liquid sealer on other parts of the fly. Sealers on rubber legs, for example, can often deform and stiffen them. To get strips with sealed or colored skins, check out Bill Skilton's USA-Flies for a list of popular beetle-like strips and materials.

Palmer tie with tip at rear for realism. Caterpillar flies often use palmered hackle as simulation for the many legs and also for the setae (fine spines) that cover the bodies of some species. Palmered hackle is best for this, with the best procedure being to tie down the tip of the hackle at the rear of the pattern, working to the front with the body material, and palmering over the body with the hackle.

You can do this with sinking caterpillars of yarn or chenille or floating caterpillars of closed cell foam. Leave the hackle as it is or clip it to give it the short spiky look of some real caterpillars. It is also possible to use short lengths of palmered hackle on both ends of the fly to simulate the front and back setae of some caterpillars.

Bluegills terrestrials on long-shank hooks. One of the problems with some fish is that they fill up their whole mouth with a terrestrial when taking the fly. This is particularly true of popular bluegills, although it is also possible with any of the sunfish including pumpkinseed, longear, redbreast, green, warmouth, rock bass, and redear sunfish.

The problem is that a terrestrial, particularly a beetle pattern, can fill up the small mouth of these fish like a wine cork stuck in a bottle. Even if the terrestrial is small, if it is taken inside of the mouth, it is almost impossible to get to and remove without hurting the fish. That's true of any fly in these fish, since the tiny mouth opening makes it tough to get straight disgorgers or hemostats into the mouth without killing it. Fingers and pliers are definitely out. Unless the hook is lodged in the lip or jaw and removable with standard fly disgorgers of any type, fly removal—including terrestrials—is difficult.

One solution lies in tying flies on hooks with longer-than-normal shanks. This is a good idea with typical sunfish flies with bulky bodies such as beetles, bees, ants, and termites. The purpose is to tie the fly as a "normal" fly on a long shank hook so that you have about one-half of the bare hook shank extended in front of the tied-fly pattern to grab and use as a lever to twist, back up, rotate, or otherwise remove the hook from the fish's mouth. Flies tied this way may be fished as any normal fly or terrestrial, except that a small surface pattern might float head down with the weight of the added hook shank in front of the fly body.

With sinking patterns, the added shank length should make little difference in casting, presentation, sinking, drifting, or fishing. Extended-shank sinking flies might sink a little faster and stay a little deeper as a result of the added shank length weight, but that would be the only effect on fishing.

Making hopper legs. Commercially sold hopper legs are now available in plastic, as well as in knotted turkey and pheasant (Rainy Riding), that you can tie in to simulate the

Use a latch hook tool (Rainy Riding) to make your own hopper legs from turkey (shown) or other feathers. Begin by holding the latch hook tool in back of a section of turkey feather as shown, with the stem of the turkey feather crushed and held in your fly tying vise for help and support.

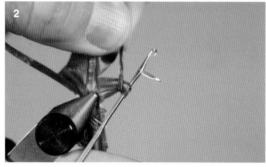

Wrap the end of the section of turkey around the latch hook tool and up over the feather section extending from the center vane.

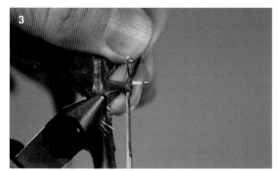

Grab the end of the feather section with the latch hook tool and then pull through to create an overhand knot. The overhand knot will create an angle in the feather which is ideal for simulating hopper legs.

Here, the end of the feather section has been pulled through the knot with the latch hook tool to make the knot necessary for the legs. Then the main part of the feather section is cut from the vane for use in tying hopper legs.

angled leg of a grasshopper. You can also make your own by using a latch-hook tool to create an overhand knot in a small bundle of feather fibers. For this, use turkey or any other long-fiber feather. One advantage of an overhand knot is that it pulls up at an angle to create the angled appearance of a natural jointed leg. These latch-hook tying tools are sold by fly shops and are available from Rainy Riding and other manufacturers.

Doubling mono/rubber strands to make hopper legs. One way to make the angled rear legs of hoppers is to use the same latch-hook tool and overhand knot techniques listed previously to first make a knot in two strands of mono or rubber legs. Then clip one strand on one side of the knot to make the lower part of the leg, using the two strands above the knot for the hopper thigh that is to be tied to the body. If using mono for this, make two overhand knots in the double mono, positioning the knots for the right length of the desired hopper thigh. This allows clipping between the two knots to make two legs. Then clip the tag end strands close to the knot to make the lower leg. To further create a natural looking leg, dip and coat the mono two-strand leg in Pliobond or similar tan contact cement. The cement can spread between the two strands to make an appropriate-size thigh that is still easy to tie down.

Use Estaz for legs on small beetles. One easy way to make legs for small beetles is to tie in a foam body at the rear of the hook shank, then wrap the hook shank with Estaz or cactus chenille, and fold over the foam to make the body and tie off. The spiky Estaz simulates legs on small beetles and ladybugs.

Tie foam parachute post for low floating ant. When ants fall into the water, they float low and in the surface film, not high as do mayflies. To simulate this, try some ant patterns with a parachute hackle tied around a thin foam post. The foam floats the fly in the surface film, and the hackle resembles legs. The low float resembles the float of live ants.

Tie calf-tail parachute post for ants. Use calf tail in bright fluorescent colors as a strike indicator/visual aid when making parachute posts on ants and other segmented flies where a low hackle is desired. Use only a short length of calf tail and a bundle no larger than necessary. The result is a more visible but low-floating terrestrial.

Adding wings to ants to make flying ants. Wings may be added to almost any ant pattern. Materials can include almost anything that would be winging material. These include craft store ribbon materials, Krystal Flash, hackle tips, hackle strands, plastic bag and wrapping materials, strands of Super Hair, thin packing plastics, various pearlescent or clear fly tying wing materials, and similar materials. The advantage of fly tying wing materials that come in sheet form is that they can be clipped and cut to size and shape for each ant or terrestrial that you are tying.

Positions of tying in ant wings. Wings may be tied down in two different spots on an ant imitation. One possibility is the junction of the abdomen and thorax. Another possibility is the junction of the head and thorax. Often the decision as to where to tie is based on the style of ant, which in turn is often based on the size of ant. Small ants usually are tied with just two body parts—the abdomen and thorax. Larger ants, including Chernobyl ants, are tied with all three body parts and any added wings secured in back of the head and with, or over, the thorax. Realize that these wings do not change in any way the use, "need," or position of legs or hackle, since these can be tied down before or after the wings are tied in place.

Often terrestrials look best with clipped hackle that will more closely resemble legs, setae of caterpillars, etc. An easy way to do this is to not clip the finished fly, but to clip the hackle to a desired length before tying it on to the terrestrial. To do this, stroke the feather toward the butt to extend the fibers and then cut as shown here.

Hackle for winged ants. White seems best when tying with hackle strands or hackle tips since it most closely approximates the silvery, shiny wings of real flying ants. Some tiers use grizzly tips. This gives the wing a mottled appearance that is less natural than the plain white hackle tips. One unusual way to make a winged ant is to use a small hackle with the fibers pulled in reverse on a short section of the center vane and tied down.

Basics of tying down ant wings. There are several basic ways in which wings may be tied down. They can be tied to lay flat on the body, or raised up at about a 45 degree angle; splayed in or flared out. The most natural wings are tied flat and slightly flared out because this most closely simulates the natural position of wings on flying ants. Wings can also be tied straight back if preferred.

Examples of clipped vs. natural hackle. Neither is "right" or "wrong;" it is only a matter of choice. Top right—natural hackle. Lower left, clipped hackle—both on fur ant patterns.

Other wings of stranded materials, Krystal Flash, cut bags, and packing material, can be tied with loops of thread around the base of each wing to splay out or extend straight back over the body.

Clipping hackle to make more realistic legs. Generally, clipping hackle for any reason other than to trim the top or bottom hackle to create a floating effect is frowned upon. The reason is that for most fly tying, the delicate tapered ends of a hackle most closely resemble the delicate legs of a mayfly, caddis fly, or stone fly. This does not apply when tying terrestrials, however, since the legs of ants, beetles, jassids, roaches, cicadas, spiders, grasshoppers, crickets, bees, wasps, and such are not tapered and delicate, but often stumpy, stick-like ,and usually blunt.

For this effect, use a longer than normal hackle and then clip it to both the right length leg and to make the leg look more realistic. This also works well when clipping palmered hackle that is spiraled around a caterpillar pattern to resemble the legs and setae found on many species.

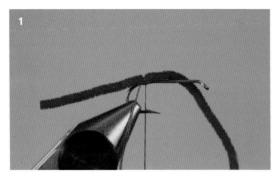

You can tie a coiled type of manure worm that will simulate what live worms do on a hook. To do this, first tie in a red chenille as shown but leave a long tag end.

Continue by wrapping over the tag end and the chenille to about ⅓ of the hook shank.

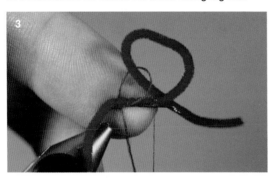

Coil the tag end of the chenille on itself as shown and then bring the tag end through the loop and around the shank as shown here. (For details see page 122)

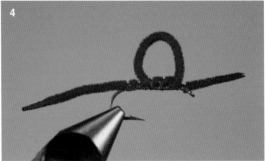

Wrap thread to the front of the hook and then wrap the tag end around the loop and hook shank to make the coil stay in place. Tie off the tag end of the thread and chenille at front of hook. Complete with a whip finish.

Circle vernille to make worms. A different way to make Vernille or Ultra Chenille red manure worms is to circle the chenille on the hook shank, just as a live worm circles and twists in the water or on the hook when it is writhing around. To do this, tie in with chenille-colored thread in the middle of the hook, leave a long tag end and wrap to the rear of the hook shank. Then tie in the chenille, allowing it to extend behind the hook. Spiral wrap over it, up to the tag end, and then go past this point by about ⅛ to ⅜ inch. Wrap over the hook shank and the chenille. Make a circle of the chenille, then wrap it in place with the tag end of thread by running the thread through the chenille circle (a latch-hook tool helps here), spiraling it and tying it off with the working thread. Continue to spiral wrap the thread over the chenille and finish the fly at the head of the hook.

Thread foam on hook to make inchworm. One easy way to make an inchworm is to use a thin green foam cylinder and thread it onto a thread-wrapped hook so that the rear of the worm extends beyond the hook shank. Tie off the inchworm at the head of the hook, or tie off at the head and allow the end of the inchworm to extend in front of the hook eye. If allowing the body to extend in front of the hook eye, a down-turned eye is best. Alternatively, tie in thread at the rear of the hook (after threading the foam on the hook) and then spiral wrap the thread over the foam and up the body. Finish by tying off at the head of the fly.

Use green-dyed feathers for spring hoppers. Grasshoppers are different colors throughout the year, and even in different geographical areas. To simulate the hoppers for your area and time of year, copy the colors of hoppers, using light green for early spring, going into darker green and then tan, yellow, and brown (mottled turkey feather) for the fall. Light green is also a good color all season for imitations of treehoppers, froghoppers, katydids, etc.

Color with felt tip pens. One easy way to make foam, balsa, and cork terrestrial patterns is to make them in white. Carry permanent felt tip markers with you in the field to color the white patterns as you fish them. I like to tie most of my flies and bugs in the finished color, but always tie and stock a few in white for coloring in the field. You can also color other body materials including yarns, stranded dubbing materials, floss, etc. Felt tip pens also work especially well on closed cell foam.

One way to mark foam bodies is to use a permanent felt tip marker. Here, a yellow Gorilla Body from Rainy Riding is being marked for a cicada killer bee pattern by using the black felt tip to make markings similar to that found on a live bee. This can be done with any shaped foam body, foam cylinder, or sheet foam.

Making color bands with felt tip markers. One easy way to make colored bands for bees, yellow jackets, and wasps is to use a cylinder or shaped yellow body and band it with a black permanent felt tip marker. To do this neatly, the best way is to secure a felt tip pen (a workshop vise is good) and then hold the yellow foam body at both ends and rotate against the tip of the pen to make a black band. This is far neater than trying to hold the pen and the yellow body freehand. Use a pen with a tip size appropriate for the band. Standard Sharpie pens are ideal for this. If you have trouble holding the foam steady for this procedure, run a needle through the cylinder axis and then rotate the foam to color it with the felt tip.

Use E-Z dub for sinking flies. One good way to tie sinking terrestrials is to use stranded dubbing materials such as Gudebrod E-Z Dub. It is available in two sizes and many colors, including some bright colors in the large saltwater series of materials that are ideal for bees, ants, wasps, and similar bright insects.

Use all sizes of vernille for worms. Most fly anglers tie only small red manure worms, using Vernille or Ultra Chenille. However, you can tie worms of any size using these same materials and in worm colors of red, brown, tan, rust, etc. Non-fly fishermen use standard earthworms in early spring to catch trout and do very well. Fly fishermen can do the same thing by fishing earthworms larger than San Juan size that are tied with large diameter chenille.

Wrap foam for floating caterpillar. One way to make a floating caterpillar is to use thin foam, tie it in at the rear, wrap the thread forward, and then wrap the foam around the hook shank to form the body complete with segmentation. If you wish to add a palmered hackle to simulate the setae, tie this at the rear when you tie down the foam body, then spiral wrap it forward.

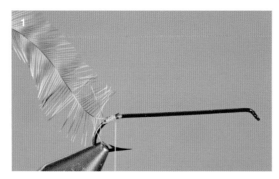

An easy way to tie a simple caterpillar is to tie in a hackle, to wrap as the setae of the insect, and to then fold a strip of foam over the hook shank. Here, in preparation of this tie, a hackle has been tied in place on the rear of the hook shank.

Begin to add the body by cutting to size a strip of foam, as with the brown caterpillar being tied here. Then fold the foam over the hook shank and tie down with spiral or sequential wraps (see text for details) around the body as you work forward.

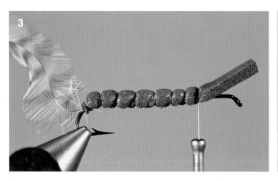

Continue tying this way towards the head of the fly as shown here.

To make it easy to tie, and to get equal segments while tying, use your thumb as shown to "mark" the position of the next wrap around each segment of the foam body.

Once the end of the hook is reached, clip and tie off the foam as shown here.

Complete the caterpillar by spiral wrapping (palmering) the hackle around the foam body as shown, and then tie off at the head of the fly. Here the completed fly is shown.

Use flash to simulate fly wings. Wings of diptera species are clear, but often create specular flashes of light. To simulate this, use a few strands of bright silver flash material (Krystal Flash, Flashabou, etc.) tied in over the back or at right angles to the body to simulate fly wings. The secret here is to use only a few short strands—instead of overkill with a large or long bundle.

Make McMurray ants with foam cylinders. Threading a needle and mono through a small balsa cylinder can be difficult. It takes time and care to prevent splitting the balsa sections used to make the abdomen and thorax of this simple ant pattern. One way around this is to use thin foam cylinders (¹⁄₁₆ inch to ⅛ inch diameter), cut to length for the abdomen and thorax.

Good dimensions are lengths equal to the diameter for the thorax, and lengths about 1½ times the diameter for the abdomen. Leave these loose so that you can position them correctly when you cut and tie down on a hook, and then cement the cylinder to the mono using cyanoacrylate glue. Colors for ant patterns include black, red, rust, maroon, and cinnamon. Use white foam for a longer abdomen when making termite McMurray patterns. Use two colored body parts followed by a white "egg case" behind the abdomen for tying egg case ant patterns. See the text on patterns for details on this.

To tie a Hewitt butterfly imitation, wrap two large oversize hackles around the center of the hook shank, each facing the center of the fly. Side view above and front view below.

Tying butterflies, Hewitt style. The Neversink Skater, developed by Edward Ringwood Hewitt, was designed in the 1930s as an imitation of a butterfly. This floating fly consists of two hackles sandwiched together to make a simple hackle fly. The pattern was a result of Hewitt's experiments with how trout see floating and sinking flies from their watery environment—involving color, refraction, and reflection of light in the trout's "window"— as well as his other experiments with fly tying, rods, reels and lines. His simple fly is described in the section on butterfly patterns on page 136.

Segmenting foam bodies on long shank hooks. Foam bodies that are no longer than the hook shank (not extended) can be segmented easily in one of two ways.

One way is to tie in the thread at the rear of the hook and then wrap one or two turns of thread in one spot over the rear of the foam body, then spiral wrap the thread around the hook shank and foam body. Work up the hook shank and tie off at the head. Because this works best with fairly tight wraps, it is best for making bodies in which the segments are small or close together. If the foam is dense, you may need heavy thread—perhaps heavier than normally used for the size fly being tied.

If making larger segments or working with larger foam bodies, first make a wrap or two of thread over one spot on the rear of the foam body. Lift the foam after each wrap to make several spiral wraps of thread around the hook shank until the thread is positioned for the next segmentation. Lower the foam on the hook shank. Make two turns of thread around the hook shank and foam to segment the body. Repeat as above until reaching the forward part of the body and tying off. This makes for a more realistic segmentation than the spiraling method, although the fish do not notice or care about the difference. The main disadvantage to the first, spiraling, method is that it can tend to twist or rotate the foam around on the hook shank, which is prevented by the second method.

Thread pressure on foam bodies. Thread pressure is important on foam bodies when tying them down, tying off, or segmenting them. With too little pressure, the foam can

Grasshoppers are tied easily on long shank hooks, using foam and segmenting them as shown in this simple completed hopper pattern. Any natural hopper color can be used including yellow, cream, tan, brown, light green, and dark green.

slide around the body and make the fly very sloppy and loose. With too much pressure, you can cut through the foam as easily as if you cut it with scissors. Usually you want moderate pressure on foam for most purposes, such as making a segmented body for a hopper or caterpillar, or segmenting a beetle. For ants, wasps, and other insects with a very thin waist, make the tightest possible wrap to compress the foam, as when making a foam style McMurray ant. It also helps to allow the thread to unwind a bit so that it becomes flat and thus will not cut as easily as would a tightly wound thread.

Segmenting folded foam strips. One way to make extended segmented dragonfly bodies is also a good way to make extended segmented bodies for hoppers, crickets, caterpillars, etc. I learned this simple technique, done off the hook and vise, from consummate tier Bill Skilton who demonstrates it extensively in his book, *My Fly Patterns, Materials and Techniques*.

To do this, first cut a long thin strip of the desired foam. Often it is best to cut these from flat sheet foam, using the thin foam (2 mm or 1/16 inch) for small hoppers, inchworms, caterpillars, etc., and the thicker foam (6 mm or 1/4 inch thick) for large hoppers, caterpillars, etc. Cut these into square strips twice the length needed for the fly body. Determine the center of each strip, then wrap and knot the tying thread around this point. Clip any excess tag end of thread.

Fold the foam over itself at this point. Bring the thread between the two pieces of foam and then close the foam around the thread. Wrap the thread twice around both pieces of foam to form a segment. Bring the thread between the two pieces of foam again, then close and wrap as above to make another segment with two wraps of the tying thread. Continue this way to make the segmented body desired.

If you find this difficult to do by hand, place a standard sewing needle in your fly vise and make these steps over the needle, removing the needle from the segmented foam body when finished.

Of course, these bodies can also be tied and segmented onto the hook. For this, segment the extended part desired, as above, freehand or on a needle. Clasp the hook shank (secured in a vise) with the two pieces of foam around the shank. Wrap the thread around the two pieces of foam and the hook shank. Continue wrapping around the hook shank only until reaching the next segment position and then make two more wraps of thread around the hook shank and both foam strips. Continue until reaching the head of the fly or completing this body segment.

It is also possible to make an extended body with the needle method of making a segmented body, then, halfway through, hold the foam around the hook shank and use the thread to tie onto the shank and complete as above.

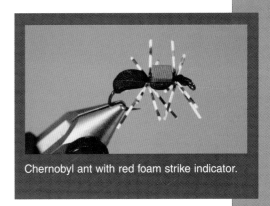

Chernobyl ant with red foam strike indicator.

Making floaters visible. There are several ways to make floating terrestrials more visible. These work on almost any terrestrial, particularly since floating terrestrials often have a body or carapace of foam, Swiss straw, Thin Skin or similar hard or sheet materials. These include:

Add a dot of paint color to the back or top of the terrestrial. For this, you can use enamel, lacquer, or fabric paint. Of these, fabric paint is the easiest, since it comes in a nozzle bottle, is easy to apply, and has some "body" that makes it stand up a little for even more visibility. Fabric paints are initially water soluble, so you must wait 24 hours after applying before fishing, at which point they are not affected by water.

Tie down a short length of glo-bug yarn with two or three turns of thread. This is usually the finishing step, after which you tie off with a whip finish. Clip the yarn short so that it stands up like a sail for increased visibility.

Glue or tie down a short rectangular length of foam in a bright color. Some foams are self adhesive stick-on, so that a small section can be stuck to the existing back or carapace of the terrestrial body. For this you must have a small section of bright self-stick foam, or you must use glue (cyanoacrylate, epoxy, or other waterproof glues) to glue the foam in place. You can also tie it down with a wrap or two of thread just before finishing the fly.

Colors of any of these—yarn, paint, or foam—should be bright, fluorescent, or day-glo colors; bright orange, yellow, chartreuse, and white are best. The one exception to this is when fishing a trout stream with bubbles and foam where white might be confused with surface foam; there, a bright orange, red, or yellow is best. In areas with a lot of glare on the water, black is best, particularly when using yarn indicators that stand up above the surface for increased visibility.

Furl chenille to make large bass-size plastic worms. Make long, larger worms that are the fly fisher's equivalent of the hardware angler's plastic worm. These are a bit of a stretch from the common insect terrestrials of a trout stream, but I am including such terrestrials for other fishing in this book.

Begin by using a length of Estaz or cactus chenille about three times the length of the worm desired. Tie in the thread at the rear of the hook and tie down the end of the chenille. With your fingers or a tool, twist the chenille in the direction in which it was wrapped during manufacture—twisting the opposite way results in the chenille coming apart or loose.

Here a set of legs is being pulled into the body with the working thread. For this step, the legs are folded over the working thread and then the thread pulled into the body to position the legs where desired.

Hold the chenille at two-thirds the length of the strand, and then fold over at the one-third point. Tie down at the two-thirds point of the chenille on the rear of the hook shank. Use a bodkin, if need be, to straighten and lengthen the twisting, furled chenille. Once the chenille is secure, wrap the thread forward to just behind the eye, then wrap the remaining chenille forward to the tie-down point, tie off, clip off any excess, and complete the fly with a whip finish. Note that you can also tie this basic pattern by adding a bead or cone head to the fly hook after bending down the point, or by adding dumb bell or bead chain eyes to the fly for weight after the rest of the fly is complete. You can also make these weedless by using several different means. My favorite is with double mono strands tied and looped onto the hook shank, then looped over the hook point to protect it, with the end of the mono tied off at the head after the rest of the fly is complete.

A handy tool for this is a Kreinik drill. This is a small plastic craft drill available at many arts and craft stores. It works like hand drills available in the days before electric drills. To make it easier to use, attach a short length of rubber hose to the end, then a hooked-in bulldog clamp available from stationery and office stores. This makes it easy to grip the material for fast twisting when tying multiples of these flies.

Use rubber legs on ants, beetles. Typical legs on ants and beetles are often wraps of hackle, sometimes strands of deer hair or wraps of Estaz and similar cactus chenille. Another way to make less bushy but more realistic legs involves tying in rubber legs at the waist of the ant or on the hook shank of beetles.

Add rubber legs to the hook shank and waist of the ant after the rest of the ant is finished. When making foam, deer hair, or similar beetles, add the legs first and then fold over or otherwise attach the foam body. The simple way to do this is to add two strands of rubber legs to each side of the hook shank and pull the thread tight, then repeat. The result is eight legs total, four on each side. (Never worry that this is more than the six legs of a real insect. Fish cannot count.) I like to keep rubber legs long, since, if necessary, they can be clipped short with scissors while fishing. The long legs make the fly a little more "jiggy" in the water.

Use deer body hair for more than just Crowe beetles. The beetle designed by John Crowe uses black or dark-dyed deer (or other body hair) tied in at the rear, pointing rearward, and then folded over and tied down at the front to make a beetle-shape and beetle-like body. You can do the same thing with deer or other body hair to make floating natural bodies of ants, grasshoppers, crickets, caterpillars, spiders, cicadas, and flies. For this, use the same techniques as when tying the Crowe beetle, but segment the body as desired. Thus, for an ant, fold the body hair forward and tie down at the center of the hook shank, then wrap forward to make a long waist and add legs as you prefer before tying the thread up to the eye and folding over the body hair and tying down to make the thorax/head. In the middle of tying this, you can add legs of rubber, deer hair, hackle, or anything else desired.

For a grasshopper, use greenish, yellow, or tan body hair and tie on a long shank hook. Tie in the body hair at the rear of the hook shank with the body hair pointing towards the rear. Then fold the body over the hook shank. You can continue by spiral wrapping the thread over the hook shank and body hair, or by wrapping over the hook shank several turns and then making two wraps in one position, over the hook shank and body hair, to make one segment. If an extended body is desired, tie down green or tan deer hair as above, then fold over a bodkin to make a long body extension, and tie down the remainder on the hook shank as above.

Continue like this—wrapping over the shank to "space" the segments—and then make two wraps over the body hair for each segment. Caterpillars, spiders, cicadas, and flies all can be built the same way, adjusting the color of the body hair, the type of body hair (coarse such as deer or fine such as antelope) based on the size of the imitation, and your personal preference.

Note that these types of hair-bodied flies are usually best in larger size imitations, simply because the size of the hair usually makes it impossible to get a natural looking fly on very small hooks. Fortunately, most of these previous suggestions—grasshoppers, cicadas, and caterpillars—are large. Ants and spiders, however, can be large or small, and require some thought as to the pattern here. For example, ants can be made as large as Chernobyl ant patterns, on size 8 or 6 hooks, or small, on size 18 to 24 hooks. The hair-bodied construction works on the large ants, but not on the tiny sizes. The same applies to spiders and also very small hoppers and crickets.

Examples of thin and fat Crowe-style deer hair ants.

Consider simple patterns in place of complex ties. There are probably a couple of dozen ways to tie and imitate each of the various terrestrial classes—ants, termites, beetles, jassids, grasshoppers, crickets, bees, wasps, hornets, inchworms, leaf hoppers, katydids, butterflies, caterpillars, worms, cicadas, and miscellaneous insects such as roaches, lightning bugs, and other terrestrial flies. In each of these, you can tie simple or complex patterns, depending upon the expected sophistication of the fish sought, your tying skill and interest, and how basic or life-like you wish your design. In some cases, the fish might indicate what you should do; as a general rule meadow-stream trout are more discerning, questioning, and suspicious than are a bed of bluegills.

One advantage of tying terrestrials (other than the obvious that they work on almost all waters for everything from trout to panfish and bass) is that they are simple to tie. You can make them complicated if you like—with bodies of deer hair, special legs, antennae, eyes, and the like—but simple flies that, in foam, fur, feathers, or synthetics, simulate the general shape, size, and color of the insect work fine. With this in mind, consider the simplest of some of the following patterns or consider reducing them even further to the basic body shape and visual characteristics of the natural. The point is catching fish—not trying to figure out if the fish thought your offering was an ant, beetle, roach, or cricket.

To make the ends tapered in inchworms and manure worms tied with Ultra Chenille, use a flame to heat the ends and taper them. This step is also aided if you roll the ends of the chenille between your fingers.

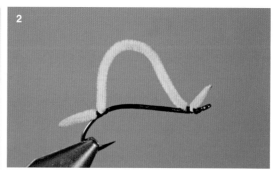

Example of inchworm with tapered ends made of Ultra Chenille.

chapter

Just why fish like to eat ants is anyone's guess. They taste (according to humans who have tried them in the ultimate dedicated research into trout foods), a little bitter and contain formic acid. Harrison Steeves III in his book (with Ed Koch) *Terrestrials*, notes that he has eaten a lot of ants of all sizes and species and finds that some are tasteless, some taste acidic, others are bitter, but all are different. Fortunately—since trout like ants a lot—they are plentiful along streams, fall into the water frequently from bank-side nests, and are fair game for fish.

According to entomology texts, there are about 15,000 ant species in North America. Imitating all of them is unnecessary, and we can reduce these to basic colors and sizes. In colors, real ants range through the spectrum of colors such as black, brown, red, and cinnamon. Ant patterns and fish interest in ants can vary from the huge that are almost impossible in nature such as the Chernobyl patterns, to the tiny as with sizes 18 and smaller for some fishing. Within all this, there are lots of different patterns, some floating and some sinking.

Often the choice of pattern is based on personal preferences, along with the size of the imitation. For example, I would not really want to try to figure out how to tie a properly proportioned McMurray ant on a size 24 hook; with small patterns, something simple does just fine. Ed Engle, in his excellent book *Tying Small Flies* (Stackpole, 2004), notes that he ties mostly simple ant patterns, because tying tiny flies on size 18 and smaller hooks prevents complexity with most patterns, including ants. Most of his ties are done with a lacquered thread body for sinking ants, and with dubbing balls or foam, for the abdomen and thorax (along with a middle wrap of hackle) for the floating patterns. They are all tied in black, red, or cinnamon colored bodies, with matching hackles.

At the other end of the scale are the huge (relatively speaking) Chernobyl ants, so named for the fanciful science fiction hypothesis of a simple ant species caught in a Russian Chernobyl toxic uranium spill genetically morphing into a huge insect. These usually are tied of foam, with separate abdomen, thorax, and head, often with more detailed legs of rubber, and with a patch of bright colored foam on top to spot them as they float down a current.

Both floating ants and sinking ants—large and small—are valuable additions to a fly box, with most anglers opting more for the floating ants than sinking patterns. The reasons are several-fold; ants (or any fly) are more fun to fish on the surface because they are more effective there (without the direct competition from aquatic insects and nymphs in the sub-surface water column), they are easier to cast and follow there, they do not have to ride high as do dry flies (so floating in the surface film is often more realistic), they are less subject to drag problems than small dry flies, and most importantly, real ants naturally float on the surface for a long time as a result of their waxy exoskeleton.

Fortunately, ants, along with other terrestrials, can be distilled into some fairly basic imitations, even though you can still end up with a variety of ways to tie them. If you look at any live ant, you have a collection of assembled parts that include a few body sections (abdomen, thorax, and head) separated by thin "waists" and six legs. I believe that the important parts of any ant imitation are the two or three body parts, the separation of these parts by "waists," and an appearance of legs—forget antennae and eyes.

You can assuredly catch fish if you exclude the legs, and you can catch fish if you forget the waist and lump the abdomen and thorax together. The only thing is that if you do that, you are really fishing a beetle and fish most likely are going to take the imitation as a beetle. If the fish still hits, how-ever, do we care what we are fishing, or what the fish thought (if it thought at all) about what it was gulping?

There is a difference in the silhouette of these floating imitations as seen by the fish. An ant will have a silhouette not unlike this: O-O-o (for the waist-separated abdomen, thorax, and head). Note that some small spiders have an abdomen not much larger than their thorax and are similar to large ants in size. Thus, they have a silhouette in size and shape similar to that of an ant. Beetles have a silhouette more like O or an oval such as a O or Oo for the long or round bulky body. The point is that if there are a lot of ants on the water, and if you want to fish an ant, then tie flies that imitate ants. Beetles and spiders are another chapter and another fly design style.

FLOATING ANTS

Foam body ants. You can tie foam ants in a variety of ways. One possibility is to use a thin foam cylinder, cut to the correct length, tied down in the center of the hook shank. Tie down just forward of center of the cylinder to separate the abdomen and thorax. By tying as tightly as possible with a wide wrap, you create the appearance of the thin waist that is characteristic of ants. Then wrap the hook shank between the abdomen and thorax with a hackle. This creates the foam equivalent of a McMurray ant. Note also that this works best with the less dense (I hesitate to say soft) foams that allow a tighter wrap at

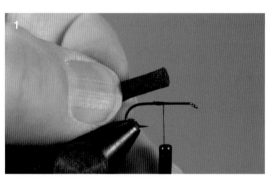

One easy way to tie a McMurray ant pattern is to use a small black foam cylinder. Begin by tying the thread in the middle of the hook shank.

Continue to tie a foam ant by tying down the foam cylinder as shown and creating a wrap with a wide waist for tying in the hackle.

Here the same is accomplished, but now with a thin, small strip of black foam. Tie in a hackle as shown.

Wrap the hackle around the waist of the ant and then tie off, as shown, to complete a simple ant.

the waist area rather than the dense foams that might be difficult to cinch up or even risk breaking the thread in doing so.

Some sample patterns include:

Foam cylinder ant, McMurray style

McMurray ants typically are made with balsa body parts threaded onto a mono core. The mono core is tied down at the center of the hook shank with the two balsa parts (abdomen and thorax) sticking up to imitate the ant body parts. You can do the same thing faster and simpler using foam cylinders.

Hook: Sizes 24 to 8
Thread: Black or to match color of ant, sized to match hook size
Abdomen: Black cylinder foam or colored foam to match that desired in ant
Waist: Thread, wrapped tight to separate abdomen and thorax
Hackle: Black or to match color of ant
Thorax: Black foam or foam to match color of ant
Tying directions: Tie down thread in the center of the hook shank, then tie down the pre-cut foam cylinder and a make tight, distinct waist with the thread. Tie in hackle, wrap hackle a few turns, and tie off. Clip excess hackle, wrap thread forward under the thorax, and tie off on the hook shank.

Variations:
Tie in any color, with red and cinnamon being popular.

Tie farther forward and secure the forward end of the foam thorax. (This is only possible in bigger ants, say size 14 and larger.)

Leave off the hackle or any legs on the very small sizes, under hook size 18.

Tie these in large sizes such as the size 8 listed and even larger to make Chernobyl ants. Often these include an extra step of tying down the foam in two places to separate the abdomen/thorax/head into the three parts. Often, too, legs are more prominent, sometimes tied in with deer hair or rubber, and some of these ants include a spot of foam glued to the top to spot them as they float.

Tie foam ants using small bits of closed cell foam that you clip from shipping insulation. Most of this is a poly cell foam—small, expanded balls that are part of the total shipping structure or sheet—which can be separated out into small "balls" of foam that

Here a foam ant with a molded-in strike indicator is tied in place. This makes a McMurray-style ant. These strike-indicator foam cylinders are available from a number of sources, including Rainy Riding and Bill Skilton USA-Flies.

The next step in tying this fly is to tie in the hackle, as shown, for wrapping the legs and completing the ant.

Here the hackle has been wrapped around the hook shank in the waist area between the front and rear of the tied-down foam cylinder.

can be tied down to make an abdomen and thorax. Other possibilities are the foam "peanuts" that are used for shipping insulation. Pinching off a bit of this material also works when tying foam ants. Most of these are light colored or white, so you have to color the foam with a permanent felt tip marker (black or red) when the tie is complete.

Example of a parachute-style cinnamon ant.

Bill's E-Z Sight Ant

This is one of Bill Skilton's patterns, although similar patterns are available using similar materials. The material is a foam cylinder in black, cinnamon, or red, with a contrasting and brightly colored end for fishing visibility. Both Bill Skilton and Rainy Riding sell such materials and they also are available in many fly shops. Most of these ant patterns are tied in black with a brightly colored tip end.

Hook: Regular hook, sizes 24 through 10
Thread: Black
Body: Black with red end foam cylinder (Bill Skilton USA-Flies E-Z Sight Foam Ant Body)
Hackle: Black dry fly hackle
Tying instructions: Tie in the thread in mid-shank, and then tie down the foam cylinder, with the bright end facing forward. Trim the rear of the cylinder if necessary. Tie in a hackle, trim the butt end, and wrap around the hook shank to make a McMurray-style foam ant. Tie off with a whip finish.

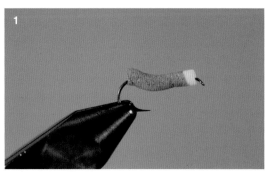

A different way of using foam cylinders is shown here with this cinnamon ant tie, using a foam strike-indicator cylinder. This cylinder has been threaded onto the hook shank.

The thread is now attached to the body and hook, as shown here, and then wrapped to make a waist for tying the hackle.

Here a ginger hackle is tied in place, for making the legs, as with a standard foam or balsa McMurray ant pattern.

This ginger hackle has been wrapped around the waist area of the fly to tie a simple ant.

Variations:

Tie with various color ends or tips. End colors include white, red, yellow, chartreuse, and orange.

You can also use longer end-color cylinders to make ants with two tie-down points and two wrapped hackles (a basic Rainy Riding/Bill Skilton style) to make an ant with separate abdomen, thorax, and head, or a larger Chernobyl style.

Ant with threaded foam body

Use thin diameter foam cylinders or bits of foam, threaded onto a hook shank to make the two parts typical of most ant patterns.

Hook: Hook sizes 20 through 8
Thread: Black or to match ant color, sized to the hook
Abdomen and Thorax: Black cylinders or foam bits, cut to abdomen or thorax length, or color desired in ant (red or cinnamon)
Hackle: Black or to match ant color
Tying directions: Cut the foam cylinders into two short lengths proportional to the hook size used. Thread these bodies, thorax first, followed by the abdomen section, onto the hook point. Slide the bodies around the hook bend to the shank and glue in place with cyanoacrylate glue. Leave a separation between the two parts. Tie down thread between the two body parts and then tie in a hackle. Wrap the hackle around the hook shank, tie off, clip the excess hackle, and complete the fly with a whip finish. Take care to not matt the hackle when pulling the whip finish tight.

Variations:

Tie in any color, with red and cinnamon being popular.

Leave off the hackle (legs) on very small flies to simplify this pattern. The fish will not mind.

In place of foam cylinders, use small bits of foam from packing materials, as mentioned above. Run preliminary tests with glues, since not all plastic foams work with all glues.

Tie in a parachute post (calf tail, right angle length of mono, hackle stem—secured between the foam sections) and then wrap the hackle around this parachute style. Use only a few wraps, since the foam floats the ant—hackle is not necessary for this. The result is an ant in which the legs more closely resemble the spread of ant legs of the live insect, with the body parts separated.

Ant with folded foam body

Use thin strips of sheet foam to make ants by tying in the foam at mid-section, then wrapping to the rear and finally folding over the foam to tie down at the waist to make the abdomen. These are just like making beetles, but with the tight and somewhat lengthened waist tie-down, at a different place, to create a waist.

Hook: Sizes 16 to 8
Thread: Black or to match ant color and sized to the hook
Abdomen and Thorax: Black (or color of preferred ant) sheet foam, cut into small strips

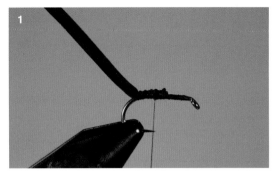

To tie a folded foam ant, first wrap on foam at the middle of the hook shank, with the foam pointed towards the rear. This prevents the foam from twisting on the hook shank.

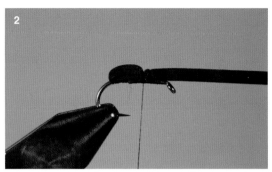

Here, the foam has been folded over and tied down at the halfway point on the hook shank to make the abdomen of the ant.

After the foam is tied down at midpoint, tie in a hackle as shown to make the legs of the ant.

Here the hackle has been wrapped around the hook shank in front of the foam abdomen to make the legs of the ant.

After tying the rest of the thread forward, the remaining foam is tied down to make the front of thorax/head of the ant pattern.

and tied in and then folded over from the rear of the hook shank before being tied down in hook center.

Hackle: Black, or color to match ant

Tying directions: Cut a thin strip of sheet foam in the color desired for the ant. Then tie on the working thread at the middle of the hook, and tie down the foam, pointed towards the rear. Wrap over the foam and hook shank towards the rear, then wrap the thread forward to the center of the hook. Fold over the foam and tightly tie it down with the thread. Wrap the thread for a short distance along the shank to make a "waist" between the abdomen and thorax. Tie in a hackle, wrap the hackle around the hook shank several times, tie off and clip. Wrap the thread forward, then tie down the foam again and clip the excess foam. Tie off the thread and clip any excess.

Variations:

Tie the ant in any color desired, with black, red and cinnamon being the best natural color choices.

Tie in the ant with no hackle at all. This is particularly good with very small ants (sizes 18 and smaller).

Tie the ant with a few strands of black deer hair tied in at the waist of the fly (center of the hook shank) to simulate the legs. Clip the legs short.

Wrap the hackle after tying down the folded foam body, then wrap the thread forward over the hook shank and tie off the forward part of the thorax before finishing the fly.

Deer hair body ants

These are tied with folded body hair (deer, antelope, caribou, etc.). In essence, these begin just like tying instructions for a Crowe beetle, but by tying a short abdomen, long waist and slightly shorter thorax/head.

Examples of thin and fat Crowe-style deer hair ants.

To tie a deer hair body Crowe-style ant, first tie in the deer hair at the rear, pointing towards the rear. Then wrap the thread to midpoint as here, and fold over the deer hair and tie down.

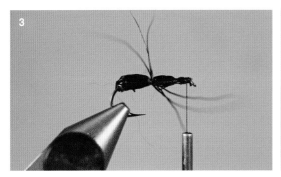

Of the remaining deer hair fibers pointing forwards, splay out a few on each side to serve as legs.

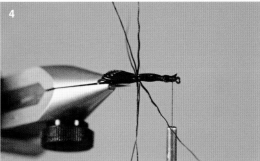

Here the fly is completed by leaving the deer hair extend from the center as legs, wrapping the thread forward, and then tying off the rest of the deer hair for the thorax and head. Clip and complete with a whip finish. The legs can be left long or can be clipped short.

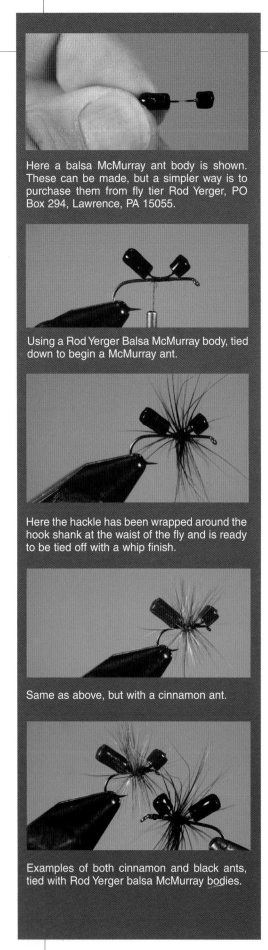

Here a balsa McMurray ant body is shown. These can be made, but a simpler way is to purchase them from fly tier Rod Yerger, PO Box 294, Lawrence, PA 15055.

Using a Rod Yerger Balsa McMurray body, tied down to begin a McMurray ant.

Here the hackle has been wrapped around the hook shank at the waist of the fly and is ready to be tied off with a whip finish.

Same as above, but with a cinnamon ant.

Examples of both cinnamon and black ants, tied with Rod Yerger balsa McMurray bodies.

Hook: Regular or 2X long hooks, sizes 16 to 8

Thread: Black

Abdomen and Thorax: Black body hair, folded over and secured with thread

Hackle/legs: Several body hair fibers, splayed out at the waist of the fly

Tying directions: Tie in at the center of the hook shank and tie in a small bundle of body hair pointing towards the rear. Wrap the thread over the deer hair to the rear then wrap the thread forward to the center of the hook. Fold over the deer hair bundle and tie down tightly. Wrap along the hook shank to make a waist and wrap the thread forward. Tease out a few fibers on each side to make legs and pull them back while folding the remaining bundle forward and tying down to make the thorax. Tie off and then clip the legs to desired length.

Variations:

Tie this with red or cinnamon body hair to make red or cinnamon ants.

Use a wrapped hackle in the middle instead of the body hair legs.

Leave off legs in the smaller sizes of flies. With hits and caught fish, legs break and work out of the body anyway.

McMurray ant

This classic design utilizes two cork, or balsa, body parts (slightly different in length—abdomen and thorax) joined on a short length of mono. Tie the mono down at the center of the hook shank and then wrap a hackle at this same point to complete this fly.

Hook: Regular hooks, sizes 16 to 8

Thread: Black or color to match ant

Body parts: McMurray body parts of balsa or cork, strung on a length of fine mono. Paint to match ant color desired.

Hackle: Black or color desired in ant

Tying instructions: All of the tying for this pattern occurs in the middle of the hook shank. Tie down the thread on the hook, then tie in the McMurray ant body. Finish by adding a hackle, wrapping it around the hook shank to make legs and then tie off. Complete the fly with a whip finish. If you do not have the McMurray body parts (they are available commercially) you can make them by using fine mono, threaded through a needle, and then threading the needle (and mono) through alternate parts of balsa cylinder for thorax and abdomen. Usually these are just slightly varying lengths of balsa or cork cylinders. Balsa and cork are ideal for this, with foam (as described previously) being another possibility.

Variations:

Tie in a parachute style, wrapping the hackle horizontally around the waist between the hook shank and the secured McMurray body parts. Tie different color ants by varying the color of the body parts and hackle.

Parachute hackle ants

This is more a variation of existing styles, rather than a new or different pattern. (Some parachute styles have been mentioned previously.) For example, tie the basic body parts of any ant pattern, add a parachute post, and then add a horizontally wrapped parachute hackle to the fly. This can be done on the top or bottom of the fly. In either case, the fly imitation floats in the surface film, rather than on it. This is closer to how an ant actually floats when it falls into the water. Since the hackle is not necessary for flotation of these mostly foam, cork, or balsa flies, hackle under the water or resembling splayed legs is not a problem.

The only disadvantage of parachutes is that by floating low and natural, they are harder to spot and follow as they drift down a trout run. A high post of colored calf tail or daub of paint or stick-on bright foam spot helps visibility.

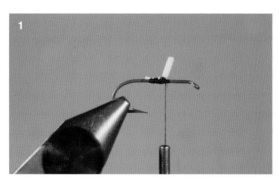

One way to tie in a post for a parachute ant is to tie in a visible strike indicator post as shown above. The next step is to tie in a foam or fur body and hackle, then wrap the hackle around the post as shown below.

It is also possible to tie McMurray-style ants with parachute hackle by wrapping the hackle around the pattern between the hook shank and the body. Here, a foam cinnamon ant with a strike indicator has been tied down and a hackle feather tied in place.

To tie a parachute hackle on a McMurray ant pattern, use hackle pliers to hold the hackle tip and wrap it around in the space between the body and hook shank.

Top view of parachute style McMurray ant, showing the body and the hackle. This style of tying often makes for an ant that floats lower in the water and also has a more realistic leg simulation than with the standard McMurray tie.

Example of parachute hackle on foam style McMurray ant.

WINGED ANTS

You can make almost any ant pattern into a winged ant by tying down wings. This is done best with floating-style ants, but can be tied with sinking ants also. This is probably least attractive or possible with McMurray-style ants, whether tied with the standard balsa or cork cylinders or with foam, or those with a hackle tied parachute style. It is easiest with those floating ants tied with threaded foam bodies, wrapped foam bodies, or foam Chernobyl ants. It is also easy with fur body and epoxied thread-wrap underwater ants. Here is a typical winged ant pattern.

Folded foam body winged ant

Hook: 2X long shank, sizes 14 to 6
Thread: Black
Abdomen and Thorax: Tie down black foam in the center of the hook shank. In larger sizes (8 and 6) this ant can also be tied with a foam head.
Hackle (optional): Black, tied at junction of abdomen and thorax
Wing: Few strands of clear or silver Krystal Flash, tied down in front of the thorax and divided at slight angle
Tying instructions: Tie in the thread in the center of the hook shank, then tie down the foam cylinder or shaped foam body to form the abdomen/thorax separation. Add a wrapped hackle and tie in the wings at this point also, flaring them back and slightly out to the side. Tie off the hackle and wings, then wrap slightly forward, and tie off and finish the fly.

Variations:
Tie in any ant color desired.
  Eliminate hackle.
  Tie wings of any appropriate material

The wings can also be tied in at the head or at the abdomen/thorax junction. This ant pattern is not complete and will have a wrapped hackle added next.

Winged ant pattern with the wrapped hackle added to complete the fly. This can also be used as a housefly pattern since they are very similar imitations.

Here an ant is being tied with the wings added to the front of the fly—just in back of the head and ahead of the legs and thorax.

Top view of winged ant with the wings added to the front of the fly.

Flash material has been used in these ant wings, tied in at the abdomen and thorax junction.

Another example of an ant, this with sheet material for wings.

Foam Chernobyl ant

These are large ant patterns, with more detail and parts than smaller ants, although they remain stylized as to the ant shape.

Hook: Regular or 2X long shank hook, size 10 to 4
Thread: Black or to match ant color
Abdomen: Black foam, tied onto the hook shank
Thorax: Black foam, with this an extension of the foam from the abdomen and tied down a second time (forward) to make three body sections
Head: Black foam, extending forward from the tie and separation of the head/thorax
Hackle or legs: Colored or black rubber legs, tied in at the two tie-down points used to separate body parts
Tying instructions: Tie in the thread at the center of the hook shank, then tie in the foam, pointed towards the rear. Wrap over the foam to the rear of the hook shank. Wrap the thread forward to the center of the hook shank and fold the foam over to tie down and create a waist. This separates the abdomen from the thorax. Tie in one or two lengths of rubber for legs on each side of this tie-down point. Lift the foam and wrap thread forward on the hook shank, then make the second tie-down of foam to form the thorax/head separation. Again, tie in legs as previously described. If necessary, clip the excess foam forward of the head.

Variations:

Tie in any ant color desired.

Wrap around the hook shank only ahead of the head and then tie down the head to finish off the fly.

Tie down wings between the head and thorax at the forward tie-down point.

A Rainy Riding style uses the above tie, but with a full body wrap of cactus or ice chenille before tying down the foam and legs. No hackle is added.

Here foam is being tied onto the hook shank to make a large size Chernobyl ant. These are large ant patterns that usually have several sets of legs and also separate abdomen, thorax, and head sections.

For this Chernobyl ant, the foam has been tied on and folded over to make the abdomen of the fly.

Mottled rubber legs are added here, pulled into the body on each side using the working thread. This keeps the legs from sticking to the sides of the fly.

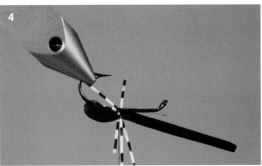

By using a rotating vise as shown here, it is easy to rotate the fly so that legs can be readily pulled into the body from each side during the tying process.

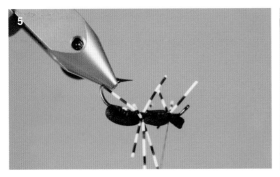

Here the thread has been wrapped forward and the second section of foam (thorax) tied down along with the first side of legs using the mottled rubber legs.

Here a set of legs is being pulled into the body with the working thread. For this step, the legs are folded over the working thread and then the thread pulled into the body to position the legs where desired.

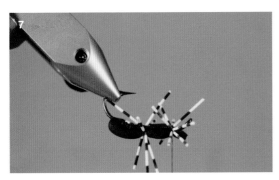

Here, all the legs have been added to the Chernobyl ant.

Chernobyl ant ready to be completed with a whip finish and tie off of the thread. Top view.

Completed Chernobyl ant, tied off and finished. Side view.

Completed Chernobyl ant, top view.

EGG (PUPA) ANT

When you accidentally or deliberately open up an ant nest, you find the small white "eggs" with worker ants tending them—usually in panic mode because you have upset their home. Usually you see ants scurrying frantically as ants carry cases in an effort to remove them from danger and protect them. While we call these white cases "eggs," they are not really eggs. Real ant eggs are much smaller. The white cases that we see and identify with are pupae or larvae of ants. These cases are often a few millimeters or more long; real eggs are about 0.5 millimeters in length (about $\frac{1}{50}$ of an inch) and almost invisible to us.

Regardless of what we call them or know about them, we can use this knowledge in our terrestrial tying. One way is to tie imitations, which include these cases in both floating and sinking patterns. I have never known anyone else to add this to an ant pattern, and my experiments with it are new, but it does deserve more testing, since in the real world it offers more of a meal—or snack—to a trout or panfish. In this, they get both an ant and a pupa, sort of the difference between a potato chip and a chip with dip.

I find it easiest to tie imitation white cases on at the rear of the fly, extending from the bend of the hook almost like a trailing shuck on an emerging trout nymph or a furled extended body fly. That is in contrast to what ants do with these when a nest is disturbed, since they carry them around by their front legs—ahead of them as we do with a shopping cart in a supermarket. The alternative in tying is to use a long shank hook and tie the ant facing front, with the case is in front of the ant and tied on the forward part of the hook shank. In tests on trout, the position of the case seems to make no difference, whether or not the ant is tied facing forward or rearward. Try both in your tying.

Other possible ties are as a McMurray style, with a white, separate case-shape on the mono core to simulate the case. The appearance that you want is one of an ant carrying and trying to care for a white case containing a pupa or larval ant. Think of these imitations more as a variation or addition to any standard ant pattern. For the case, consider any of the materials that you might use for an emerging shuck case when tying trout flies. Thus, you can use tied and folded white-colored Antron yarn, furled yarn, bits of white foam packing material, or similar foam products tied on as cases.

If tying on a long shank hook in front of a standard ant imitation, best results come from a case-shaped wrap of white floss, although a wrap of Vernille, thin band of Teflon tape, or tight-wrapped white yarn also works. Note that if you are tying these on the rear of the hook shank or as a trailing shuck style, you should adjust the ant tie so that the head/thorax is touching the case, which is how ants carry pupa.

Floss egg ant. Tied with a floss case in front of or behind the ant, using a long shank hook and tying the ant body and the case onto the hook. You can tie this with a floss case and foam ant body for a floating ant, or all floss or thread for a sinking ant.

Extended-body egg case ant. On the rear of the hook shank, tie in a short section of white foam as a case, then tie down the black foam for the ant head/thorax, wrap the thread forward, and fold over to tie down in the center of the hook with the abdomen extending forward.

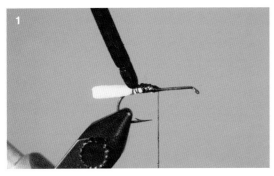

Tying a foam ant with egg case, by first tying down an extended white foam "egg case," then at the same spot tying in a black foam body.

To continue to tie this ant, tie the thread forward and then fold over the body and tie down.

Tie in a hackle for wrapping around the body to make legs for the ant.

Here the hackle has been wrapped around the hook shank to make the legs for the ant.

Here the foam has been clipped and the thread wrapped forward after tying off the hackle.

To complete the ant pattern, tie down the foam at the head of the hook in back of the hook eye. Then tie a whip finish to complete the fly.

Tying an egg case ant with the egg case at the front of the fly involves first tying the fly on a long shank hook. Once the rest of the ant fly is complete, tie in the white stranded material as shown here.

Next, wrap the stranded white material to the forward part of the fly and back for tying off at the black/white junction.

Trailing-shuck-style egg case ant. Tie in a short length of white Antron yarn, then twist to furl it (twist as per the original manufacture) to make a short "case." Tie in, and tie down the ant material and complete the fly as per any standard pattern with the furled Antron making an extended body—or a white ant case on this pattern.

McMurray egg ant. Make McMurray-style bodies, by using successive sections of two black bodies (head/thorax and abdomen), then a white body case, and repeated along a length of fine mono. Clip off a black body/blackbody/white case section for each fly, and tie down and complete as per any McMurray style.

Foam egg case ant. Thread successively three separate bodies onto a hook shank, including a white case, then a short black foam head/thorax, followed by a slightly longer abdomen. Glue with cyanoacrylate glue and then wrap hackle as desired.

Note that any of the above can be tied in any color of ant, although the case stays white in all imitations.

UNDERWATER ANTS

A number of styles are possible with sinking ants, including making winged or non-winged ants tied with fur, synthetic dubbing, thread-body, chenille-body, bead-body ants, epoxied ants, peacock herl-bodied, yarn-bodied, etc.

To tie a furled body underwater (non-floating) "egg case" ant, make a furled rear of stranded body material (EZ-Dub or yarn as shown) and wrap in place at the rear of the hook shank.

Continue the egg case ant by then wrapping in body or stranded material or yarn. For this ant, EZ-Dub has been used.

Any type of legs can be added to these or other ant patterns. For this fly, we are adding several strands of black deer hair, using a rotating vise to position the hook for pulling the deer hair into the body with the tying thread.

Dubbing body or fur body ant

Tie this ant body with dubbing or stranded fur/synthetic material. Wrap onto the hook shank, making it longer and larger for the rear abdomen than for the front thorax. Finish with a wrap of hackle, a parachute hackle, or a few strands of deer hair for legs.

Hook: Regular or 2X long hooks, sizes 18 to 8

Thread: Black or to match color of the ant

Abdomen: Black dubbing or synthetic/natural body material such as Gudebrod E-Z Dub

Thorax: Black dubbing or synthetic/natural body material

Hackle: Black, or to match the ant color

Head: Wrap of thread

Tying instructions: Tie in thread on the rear of the hook shank, then tie in the abdomen material or make a dubbing strand or loop. Wrap the thread forward. Wrap the body material around the hook shank on the rear half of the hook shank, then tie off and make a waist with the thread. Tie in a hackle, wrap, and tie off to make legs. Continue to tie in a thorax with dubbing or strand of synthetic material, then tie off and complete the fly with a whip finish.

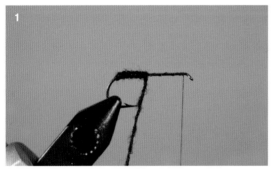

A simple fur body ant can be tied with dubbing, or stranded material as shown. The thread has been tied on and stranded body material wrapped up and tied off after the thread is wrapped to the midpoint.

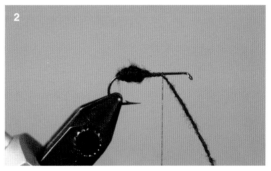

Here the thread has been wrapped forward slightly to create a waist area for wrapping hackle.

Here the body material has been wrapped forward, to tie the head and thorax, and then wrapped back for tying off at the waist area.

To complete the fly, tie in a hackle at the waist area for wrapping around the hook shank for legs.

With the legs wrapped in place, the finished fur ant is shown.

Variations:

Tie any color of ant by using different color thread, body, and hackle materials.

Tie in a few strands of deer body hair at the waist to make legs in place of the hackle.

Floss ant

Floss makes a nice, smooth, round, and life-like body for an ant, especially when coated with epoxy. The technique for tying is the same as for sinking thread body patterns.

Hook: Regular or 2X long, sizes 20 to 8
Thread: Black, or color to match ant
Abdomen: Black floss, or color to match ant
Hackle: Black, or color to match ant
Thorax: Black floss, or color to match ant
Tying instructions: Tie in thread, then tie in floss, wrap the thread forward to the waist area, and use floss to build up the abdomen. Tie down the floss and wrap a hackle. Wrap the thread forward followed by a wrap of floss and tie off. Coat the body parts with head cement or epoxy, being careful to avoid the hackle; or, tie a bunch of ants with the thorax and abdomen only, epoxy first and then later finish each fly with a hackle wrap around the center.

Variations:

Any color of floss to make any color of ant.

Tie small sizes without hackle.

Tie with deer hair for legs, tied in at the waist.

Use fine black rubber legs on larger ants, tied in at the waist after the fly is tied and epoxied.

Tie with yarn or synthetic dubbing strands in place of floss, but do not coat with epoxy.

Thread ant

Using thread for the body is best when tying very small ants, although it can be used for larger ant patterns as well. The advantage for small flies is that no additional body material is added to build up the small body required. The disadvantage, for larger ants, is that thin thread takes a lot of wraps to build up the necessary body. Simpler ways to make bodies on larger ants include using floss.

Hook: Regular hooks, sizes 24 to 14. Larger also possible, but takes more thread wraps
Thread: Black, sized to hook, or color to match ant desired
Abdomen: Wrap of thread to build up longer and fat abdomen
Hackle: Optional on small ants. Hackle wrapped around hook shank
Thorax: Wrap of thread to build up thorax
Tying instructions: Tie in thread at rear of fly, then wrap and build up the abdomen. Make a long, skinny waist, add a hackle (optional) if desired, and then build up the thread to form the thorax. Tie off with whip finish. Coat the body with several coats of head cement.

Variations:
Tie in any color desired.

An alternative to the head cement coatings is to use one coat of epoxy. Rotate fly to prevent sagging. This makes for a nice, shiny, and durable body.

If you have problems with keeping the epoxy from ruining the hackle, make up a number of fly bodies, epoxy, and rotate, then finish later with a wrap of hackle or other legs added to the fly.

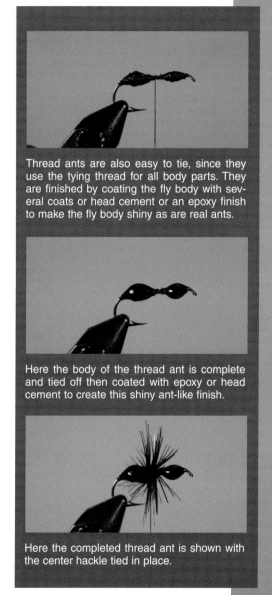

Thread ants are also easy to tie, since they use the tying thread for all body parts. They are finished by coating the fly body with several coats or head cement or an epoxy finish to make the fly body shiny as are real ants.

Here the body of the thread ant is complete and tied off then coated with epoxy or head cement to create this shiny ant-like finish.

Here the completed thread ant is shown with the center hackle tied in place.

TERMITES

As with ants, termites are a large part of the natural world. They inhabit rotting logs found along streams, lying over and in streams, and throughout the woods. Just because they invade our homes as unwanted guests does not mean that they are not even more prevalent outdoors, or that they are not good terrestrials to imitate for fishing. Since termites use wood as a cellulose food base, the best places to find them and for trout to seek them as an occasional food is in streams that have wooded banks, and where clear cutting or forest "grooming" has not removed old or dead trees but instead allowed them to lay where they fall to rot and disintegrate. The result is termites, along with a lot of other insects and similar creatures that make up terrestrial trout food.

One simple way to think of termites is to envision them as "white" ants, but with a longer abdomen and slightly thicker waist. That makes tying them easy, since all you have to do is to switch colors to white from the black, red, or cinnamon that you would use for ants and tie in a longer abdomen. In some cases, this means using a longer hook shank, such as a 2X to 4X long shank. Make longer abdomens by using a longer length of foam, tying a longer body of chenille, yarn, floss, or thread onto the hook shank.

The same applies to making a longer furled body as an extended body or trailing shuck design, such as is called for with the ant case patterns previously described. One of my favorite techniques is using plumber's white Teflon tape as a wrap on a long shank hook, ribbed and secured with white thread or clear mono. This has a glossy finish that is not unlike the body of a termite and is easy to tie and use.

To tie a furled body termite, first furl the white abdomen and then tie down, followed by tying in a white hackle and hackle wrap at the center of the hook shank. Leave the remaining stranded body material to be wrapped around the hook shank for the thorax and head.

Complete furled body termite pattern with thorax and head wrapped around the hook shank.

It often helps to have a thread base before tying down a fly tied of foam. Here, a white thread base is being prepared for a segmented, foam termite pattern.

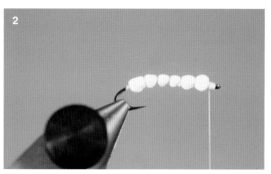

Here, white foam has been tied up the hook shank to make the segmented foam body.

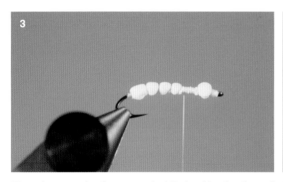

To make room for the wrap of white hackle, the thread has been reversed slightly to make a thin section for tying down the legs.

Here the white hackle has been tied down and wrapped to make the white legs of this foam termite fly. The fly is ready to be completed with a whip finish.

Another way to make a long abdomen is to make a furled body of yarn, EZ-Body, or even floss that twists on itself to create a long body. Floss tends to fray and ravel quickly though. In all these ties, use white thread.

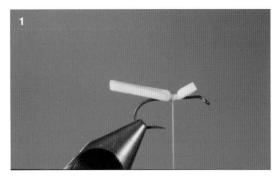

Making a foam termite is easy, since you use the same materials and techniques as when tying ants, except using white materials. Here, a white foam body is tied for a termite equivalent of a foam McMurray ant.

Here the simple McMurray-style termite with foam body has been completed by tying in a white hackle.

Foam termite. Tie as a foam ant (see previous), only use all-white materials such as white foam and a white or grizzly hackle.

Furled yarn termite. Use white yarn or synthetic stranded material to make an extended furled abdomen and wrapped thorax/head. Do this by wrapping down the thread on the rear of a regular shank hook or center of a longer shank hook. Furl (twist) the material, fold it over itself and tie down again in the same spot. Tie in and wrap a white hackle. Wrap the thread forward to the eye, then wrap the remaining material around the hook shank and tie off. Complete with a whip finish.

Tape termite. For this tie, cut two strips of Teflon tape so that the width of the cut is equal to the length of the abdomen and thorax of the termite being tied. Wrap (in the same direction as you would thread) Teflon strips around the hook shank for the abdomen and thorax, then tie on at the rear of the hook, and spiral wrap over the abdomen. Tie in a hackle and wrap, and then continue to spiral wrap over the thorax to complete with a whip finish. Tape termites, with other leg options, are tied similarly.

Floss termite. Wrap the thread onto the hook, then tie in floss and wrap the thread forward. Wrap the floss around the hook shank to form an abdomen, then tie in legs or a white hackle, finish the hackle wrap and then wrap the thread forward, followed by the floss thorax body. Complete with a whip finish.

McMurray termite. McMurray termites are tied the same as McMurray ants, except that white foam, balsa or cork bodies are used, along with a white hackle. Can be tied in any color of ant, although the case stays white in all imitations.

To tie a folded-foam body termite, tie down a white foam strip as you do with a black ant body and then fold it over. Here the foam has been tied down and is pointing towards the rear.

Fold over the foam to make the rear body of a termite as shown here.

Legs in termites can be made of many materials, as they can be with ants, with these legs made of pulled-in dyed white deer hair fibers.

Top view of the foam termite with the deer hair tied in place.

Here the deer hair has been trimmed to make for more realistic, life-like legs on this termite pattern.

Completed termite, side view.

One different way to make shiny body terrestrial patterns is with liquid coatings. This termite body has been made with white liquid electrical paint, dabbed on to the hook shank and then cured and completed with a hackle tied in place.

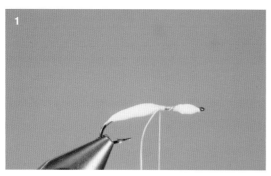

Here, the body or white liquid electrical paint is cured and the thread tied in place to add the hackle.

Hackle tied in place on termite fly pattern and ready to be wrapped.

Here the hackle is being wrapped around the hook shank in the waist area of the termite fly.

Termite fly with hackle wrapped in place, ready to be completed with a whip finish.

chapter

There are more beetles than ant species—about 30,000 beetle varieties—in the U.S. They vary widely in size, shape, and color, and so allow for a wide variety of tying styles. They are often among the best of terrestrials to use, since they offer a larger meal or snack to fish than do ants or many favored aquatic insects. Using the same materials as with ants, beetles can be tied in floating or underwater forms. These include closed cell and open cell foams, deer hair, yarn, dubbing, Swiss straw, sheet plastics, etc. The basic difference between beetles and ants is that beetles are often fatter, larger, flatter, chunkier, and sometimes come in bright or muted greens, bronzes, or other shades. Many beetles have wings covered with wing cases, which in imitations can be simulated with opaque, iridescent materials.

Some beetle patterns are even simpler than the foam and deer hair styles that are standard. One example is the jassid (also sometimes tied as an imitation of a leaf hopper) as developed by Vince Marinaro. It is nothing more than a jungle cock nail tied down over a clipped palmered hackle. Many other beetles are tied like ants, only with one major section for the body and perhaps a small head. Legs can variously be hackle, deer hair, cactus chenille, palmered hackle, etc.

While most ants and bees are similar with top and bottom colors, this may not be the case with beetles. This beetle is a dark mottled brown on top . . .

. . . and a chalky white on the bottom. When tying beetles in particular, pay attention to their belly colors before designing flies.

FLOATING BEETLES
Coffee Bean Beetle

Beetles of coffee beans seem to be a natural. Coffee beans are about the right size and shape of fat beetles, at least most common beetles and the Japanese beetles for which the beans were probably first used as an imitation.

There are fewer Japanese beetles now—and fewer bean imitations used—but the concept is still a good one. These are fragile, so it is easy to cut or split a bean in half when sawing a slot with a hacksaw; however, beans are cheap. Most grocery stores sell whole beans and various flavors range from almost black to light brown in color. These are a little more difficult to cast, since they are essentially solid, heavier than most flies, and without the feathers and fur that slows the mass/air resistance ratio that we expect with most fly-casting. The lacquer or head cement coating on these is not required, although it does help to toughen them a little. Just make sure to do it before gluing the hook into the coffee bean slot. Bean beetles are fun to tie, fun to fish, and they do fool trout and panfish.

Coffee Bean Beetle

Hook: Regular hook, sizes 12 and 10, based on size of coffee bean used

Legs: Black cactus chenille, Estaz, hackle, clipped hackle, or deer hair

Body: Lacquered coffee bean

Tying instructions: Prepare coffee bean by slotting the bottom with a fine tooth hacksaw blade. Coat with clear lacquer or head cement and allow to dry. Place hook in vise, tie down thread, and tie in and wrap leg material. Tie off and complete with a whip finish. Mix five-minute epoxy and add to slot in coffee bean, then place the wrapped hook carefully in slot. Do several of these at a time, checking as the glue cures to make sure that the hook does not rotate in the slot.

Variations:

Use black or brown coffee beans, as desired.

If desired, tie a wid,e flat braid or iridescent ribbon at the rear of the hook shank, then prepare the hook and beetle as previous. Pull the braid or ribbon over the body of the bean and tie down at the head of the fly. This makes for an iridescent beetle back (wing case) as found on many Japanese beetles and other beetles.

Add a spot of bright fluorescent fabric paint to the top of the bean for fishing visibility.

One simple way to tie beetles is to use coffee beans as shown here. Slight variations in size and color are available at your local grocer.

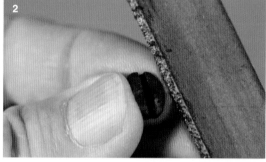

To prepare a coffee bean beetle, choose an even, smooth bean and then slot the bottom using a hacksaw blade as shown here.

Once the bean is prepared, tie on a length of cactus chenille to the rear of an appropriate hook as shown here. Then wrap up the thread followed by the cactus chenille and tie off to make "legs" for the pattern.

Prepare the bean for gluing, then add a small amount of waterproof glue to the prepared slot.

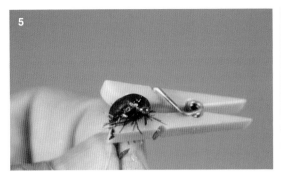

Glue the wrapped hook into the slot in the bean and then clamp with a clothespin. Best clamps are those that are baby doll clothespins as shown here.

Finished bean fly that is nothing more than wrapped legs and a body glued on a coffee bean.

Top view of a coffee bean beetle, here tied with legs of hackle in place of the cactus chenille.

To protect the bean and to make it shiny as are some beetles, add a coat of head cement as shown here. Take care to not touch the legs when doing this step.

To add a strike indicator marker on a coffee bean beetle, try using fabric paint. The best are those that come with a thin nozzle Use bright paint and allow to cure.

Completed coffee bean beetle with indicator mark.

Examples of two coffee bean beetles. Top, one tied with hackle legs. Bottom, one tied with deer hair legs.

Crowe Beetle

One of the original beetle patterns, this was developed by John Crowe and is tied of one material—deer hair. The concept is simple. It is a body of deer hair, with strands of deer hair frayed out for legs. These can be made on any size hook, simulate any size beetle, and made fat or thin, short or long, depending upon the shank length (regular, 2X or 4X long) used.

Hook: Size 22 to 8, regular or long-shank hook
Thread: Black, or to match the deer hair and beetle color
Body: Deer hair (caribou, coastal deer, elk, depending upon the fly size and the thickness of hair desired. Black is basic, but any color can be used.
Legs: Deer hair fibers, teased out from the body, and tied down to secure
Tying directions: Tie in the thread at the bend of the hook, then tie down a small bundle of hair. Wrap the thread forward to a slight distance behind the hook eye. Fold over the deer hair bundle, then tie down with the thread. You can pull on the deer hair bundle to make for a thin body, or leave it loose to make for a bulkier, fatter body. Pull out a few deer hair fibers on each side as legs and clip the rest of the deer hair short. Trim the legs and tie off the fly with a whip finish.

Variations:

Tie in any color.

For larger flies, consider a body wrap of Estaz to simulate legs, prior to folding over the deer hair to make the back.

Use fabric paint to make a small dot or bright, fluorescent color on the back of the fly for easy visibility while fishing.

Side view of finished Crowe-style deer hair beetle.

Making a deer hair Crowe-style beetle begins with tying in a bundle of black deer hair as shown.

One way to tie legs on a Crowe-style beetle is to wrap the thread forward over the excess deer hair and then splay out fibers at the front of the fly.

Here, deer hair fibers have been splayed out to tie legs in the front of this beetle fly.

Top view of the Crowe-style beetle with the legs splayed out and the body yet to be folded and wrapped forward.

Here the rear bundle of deer hair has been folded forward and tied down with the legs still splayed out to the side.

Top view of the beetle before the forward head is tied off.

Top view, here with the legs clipped to make them more life-like.

Top view of finished Crowe-style deer hair beetle.

Foam Beetle

Simple beetles of any color and design can be made easily with nothing more than a strip of foam and some cactus chenille. Additions to make them more life-like, or to fit a particular beetle shape and design, can include a wing case or back material of Thin Skin, Swiss straw, flat braid, or similar material, along with legs/antennae of hackle, deer hair, teased out braid, etc. They can be tied small or large, thin or fat, long or round, and in any color. What follows is for a simple black beetle.

Hook: Size 16 to 12 regular or 2X long shank hook for most beetles. Longer shank hooks best for click beetles, longhorn beetles, and similar long-body beetles.
Thread: Black, or matching the beetle color.
Legs: Black, dark green, or peacock Estaz or cactus chenille
Body: Foam; cut and thickness appropriate to size and shape of beetle. Bill Skilton's USA-Flies foam is ideal for this.
Back (optional): Thin Skin, wide flat braid, Swiss straw, or similar thin carapace-type material
Antennae (optional): Deer hair, rubber legs, teased-out braid, hackle, etc.

Another type of simple foam beetle that is easy to tie, beginning with a wrap of foam, with the main part of the foam pointed to the rear and ready to be folded over the hook shank to make the body/wing case.

After tying in the foam wing case, tie in the material for the body. In this case, peacock herl is being used. Other legs and body possibilities include palmered hackle, cactus chenille, or similar materials.

Once the thread is wrapped forward, wrap the peacock forward to tie the legs or body as shown here. Leave two strands of peacock herl on each side of the body for legs when trimming the peacock.

Top view of the body and legs with the foam ready to be folded and wrapped in place.

Hoppers vary from spring through fall, in both color and size. Hoppers hatch in the spring and are small, growing and often changing color as the season progresses. They usually start out a light green, although this varies with the many species found in North America. As summer progresses, hoppers grow larger and get darker, varying from the light green or yellow of early spring to a darker or mottled yellow/tan/brown of mid- to late-fall.

If you are serious about your hopper fishing or if hoppers are plentiful where you fish, tie and stock a series of hoppers that cover both size and color variations. Hoppers can be tied from about size 14 up through about size 6 or even 4 hook, usually on a 2X to 4X long hook to compensate for the extra length of these insects. It also helps to tie some in light green, using dyed quill wings for the folding hopper wing along with some matching yellow or light green dyed deer hair (or other body hair) where suggested in the pattern. For late summer and fall hoppers, tie patterns with yellow, dark yellow, or orange bodies and with yellow, tan, or brown wings. Natural or dyed deer or antelope hair is often good for this. For fall in particular, I like mottled turkey feathers for hopper wings, since they closely simulate the mottled wings and bodies of the real thing. Just realize that you do not have to go too far as to exact imitation of hoppers and various crickets. For example, crickets have cerci (projections), one each sticking out at an angle from their abdomen rear and female crickets have a long black ovipositor extending from the center rear (between the cercus) to deposit eggs; neither of these is necessary in cricket imitations. I think that most fish are going after the general appearance of the cricket, do not care about any details and especially do not know or care about which gender they are eating.

FLOATING HOPPERS, CRICKETS

Goose Quill Hopper

I developed this pattern some 55 years ago, although as fly patterns go, I am sure that others invented it long before me. It is a simple basic design—cut off the appropriate length of a goose quill end, plug the end with glue or a small cork, wrap it onto a hook shank, paint it and add legs or hackle. The hollow goose quill floats, making this an ideal grasshopper or cricket (if painted black) imitation. It was particularly good in those early 1960s before the extensive development of foam for floating bugs. It is far more fragile than the foams of today, although I still like to tie, keep on hand, and fish with them now and again.

Hook: 2X to 3X long, sizes 10 to 4
Thread: White, then light green thread or thread, to match quill body color
Body: Butt end of goose quill, cut and plugged
Legs: Green rubber or green-dyed deer hair
Hopper Legs: T.N.T. hopper legs
Tying instructions: Cut and sand the end of a goose quill, then plug it with a tiny cork (trimmed) or blob of epoxy. Tie the thread in mid-shank and then tie down the quill body, wrapping over the hook shank and quill along the full length of the hook shank. Tie off and paint green, light green, tan, or brown, depending upon season and color of hopper desired. Allow to cure and then retie around quill with color thread to

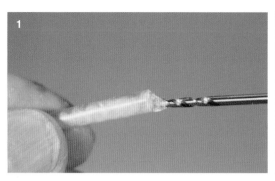

To tie a quill hopper, first get a quill from a goose, turkey, or other large bird. Cut the quill to the length desired and sand smooth. Use a drill bit or small hook to clean out the hollow body of the quill.

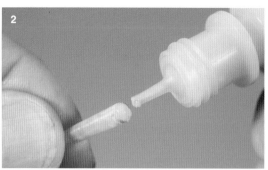

Seal the open end of the quill with glue or thick fabric paint as shown here. Another possibility is a tiny cork, glued in place and then sanded flush.

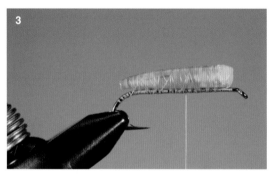

To tie a quill body hopper, tie the prepared hopper body (quill) onto the hook. It also helps to use a little glue to help stabilize it in place. After it is tied on, it will be painted.

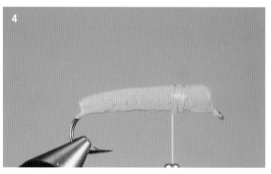

This quill has been tied to the hook shank and then painted. This is the second step in which the thread is being attached to the quill body for adding legs.

After the thread has been tied onto the quill body, the next step is to tie in legs. Many leg materials can be used—in this case, the legs are dyed deer hair matching the color of the painted quill body.

To complete the hopper, rear legs are added. Options are available for these also. These legs are life-like molded T.N.T. legs that are tied in place and which closely resemble rear hopper legs.

match painted quill body. Wrap back to about ⅓ to ½ from the hook eye, and then tie in hopper legs, one on each side. For additional legs, tie in deer hair or rubber legs on each side and trim to resemble hopper legs. Tie off with a whip finish.

Variations:

Paint up all the quill bodies first—and then tie on and wrap in place with tying thread that matches the quill body color. That way, no painting must be done of each tied hopper. This makes for easier, quicker, tying.

In place of paint, use a permanent opaque felt tip marker to color the wrapped quill body after tying down the body and before tying on the hopper and other legs.

Substitute knotted feather legs, knotted rubber legs, or similar hind legs as desired.

LeTort Hopper

This fly, developed by Ernie Schwiebert, is a variation of some earlier hopper flies. It was developed on the limestone LeTort, a Pennsylvania trout stream that was a laboratory for many fly pattern developments, including many terrestrials. It is one of several hoppers listed here, and a good one that is simple to tie and effective to use.

Hook: 2X long, sizes 12 through 6
Thread: Yellow
Body: Yellow fur dubbing or yellow synthetic dubbing
Wing: Brown mottled turkey feather, lacquered
Collar: Tips of brown deer hair, tied long
Head: Trimmed deer hair

Tying instructions: Tie in the thread at the midpoint of the hook shank and then tie down the synthetic dubbing or make a dubbing loop and wrap. Tie the thread forward to about ⅓ behind the hook eye. Work the dubbing back and forth on the hook shank to build up the body along the length of the hook. Tie off at the thread. Cut and tie down a section of turkey feather to make a wing that extends just in back of the hook shank. Prepare a bundle of deer hair, remove the underfur, and tie down so that the tips extend to the rear. Tie tight to make a flared head and trim the head to finish the fly. Tie off with a whip finish.

Variations:

You can also tie a slim and small version of this to simulate a leaf hopper, using a light green body wrap, light green quill wing, and light green deer hair.

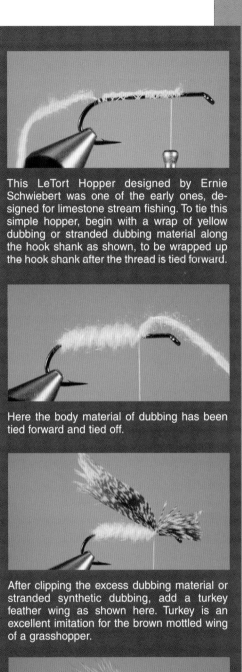

This LeTort Hopper designed by Ernie Schwiebert was one of the early ones, designed for limestone stream fishing. To tie this simple hopper, begin with a wrap of yellow dubbing or stranded dubbing material along the hook shank as shown, to be wrapped up the hook shank after the thread is tied forward.

Here the body material of dubbing has been tied forward and tied off.

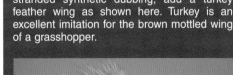

After clipping the excess dubbing material or stranded synthetic dubbing, add a turkey feather wing as shown here. Turkey is an excellent imitation for the brown mottled wing of a grasshopper.

Complete the fly by adding a wing and collar of deer hair as shown. Make sure that the tips are to the rear and trim the collar as you would a Muddler Minnow.

To tie an Ed Shenk LeTort Hopper, first tie in a length of synthetic dubbing (EZ-Dub here) and then wrap the thread forward followed by the wrap of body material.

Tie in a turkey feather section with it flat on top of the body as shown.

Angled view of above.

Add a wing of deer hair in natural brown or tan color. This bundle can be full (as is shown here) or sparse as you wish.

Trim the head to complete the fly as shown.

Underside of the Shenk LeTort Hopper—the fly as the fish would see it.

Shenk LeTort Hopper

Ed Shenk developed this early hopper pattern. It is simple and effective on all waters, and can be modified easily as to color and size.

Hook: Hook 2X long in sizes 16 to 10
Thread: Yellow or to match the hopper color
Body: Spun fur in colors yellow, cream, tan, or orange
Wing: Section of turkey feather, folded and tied flat with the tip trimmed to a broad "V"
Hackle: Tips from the deer hair head, trimmed on the underside
Head: Spun tan deer hair
Tying instructions: Tie on the thread at the rear of the hook shank and then prepare the spun body and tie down as you work to the front of the hook. Tie off any excess spun fur and add a folded and trimmed turkey feather section for the wing. Add and tie down a small bundle of deer hair, with the tips towards the rear. Trim the deer hair on the underside of the fly and trim the butt ends into a head. Tie off and complete with a whip finish.

Variations:

No variations, since that would change this basic hopper pattern into something else and would not be Shenk's pattern.

LeTort Cricket

This pattern, developed by Ed Shenk, is a cricket variation of the previously described LeTort Hopper.

Hook: Sizes 12 to 8
Thread: Black
Body: Black synthetic dubbing or dubbing loop
Wing: Black wing quill section
Collar: Black deer hair
Head: Black deer hair, trimmed

Example of a Ed Shenk LeTort cricket. This is tied just as is the hopper, only using all black materials.

Tying instructions: Similar to the LeTort Hopper. Tie in at the midpoint of the hook, tie in the synthetic dubbing, and wrap the thread slightly forward. Work the dubbing back and forth on the hook shank to build up a body. Tie off and clip excess. Prepare and tie down a wing of black quill feather. Trim any forward excess. Prepare (remove underfur) and tie down a bundle of black deer hair with the tips pointing to the rear. Trim the butt ends to make the collar.

Variations:
Tie in all brown materials to simulate a mole or camel cricket.

Begin Joe's Hopper by tying in a tail of red hackle fibers, adding a yellow synthetic stranded body.

Add a hackle as shown for palmering up the body of the fly.

Wrap the synthetic body material forward and tie off and clip as shown here.

Palmer the hackle up the fly body, spiraling it over the body as shown and tying off a little behind the head.

Tie off the materials in back of the head, leaving enough room to add the turkey wing and the hackle.

Next, add a turkey feather wing to the fly, placing it on top of the body as shown.

Tie in a tan, brown, or ginger hackle as shown for wrapping around the fly to nearly complete it.

Here the fly is complete before tying off the hackle, clipping the excess, and finishing the fly with a whip finish.

Joe's Hopper

This is one of the early and original hopper patterns that is primarily a western style, but which can be used anywhere and adjusted by size to local conditions.

Hook: Regular or 2X long hook, sizes 18 through 6
Thread: Brown
Tail: Red goose quill or red deer hair
Body: Yellow yarn—wool or synthetic
Rib: Brown or ginger hackle
Wing: Turkey quill section
Hackle: Mixed ginger/brown and grizzly
Tying instructions: Tie in the thread, then tie back to tie in the tail and the hackle ribbing. Wrap forward to the middle of the shank, and tie down the body. Wrap the thread forward to about ⅓ of the way behind the hook eye. Wrap the body material back and forth to build it up and tie off with the thread. Palmer the ribbing hackle forward and tie off. Prepare and tie down a section of lacquered turkey quill for the wing. Tie in grizzly and ginger or brown hackles and wrap to make the hackle. Tie off and complete with a whip finish.

Variations:

You can change any of the materials or colors of this fly, but that would then change it from a specific pattern of Joe's Hopper to a variation or some other pattern or style of hopper.

Dave's Hopper

The main difference between this hopper by Dave Whitlock and Joe's Hopper is the use of deer hair in place of a hackle for the finish of the fly. The rest—tail, body, ribbing, and wing are all the same. Nevertheless, both flies have their adherents and both work well. They are particularly popular on midwestern and western waters.

Hook: Hooks 2X long, sizes 14 through 6
Thread: Brown
Tail: Red deer hair
Body: Yellow wool yarn
Rib: Brown hackle
Underwing: Pale yellow deer hair
Wing: Section of turkey wing quill
Collar: Brown deer hair
Head: Deer hair, trimmed
Tying instructions: Tie in the thread, then tie back to tie in the tail and then the hackle ribbing. Wrap forward to the middle of the shank, and tie down the body, then wrap the thread forward to about ⅓ back from the hook eye. Wrap the body material back and forth to build it up and tie off with the thread. Palmer the ribbing hackle forward and tie off. Prepare and tie down a section of turkey quill for the wing. Prepare (remove underfur) and tie down a bundle of deer hair with the tips pointing towards the rear. Trim the butt ends to form the head, then tie off with a whip finish.

To tie a deer hair hopper, begin by first tying on the thread and then tying down a bundle of deer hair as shown, with the main part of the bundle pointed towards the rear.

Continue to tie by folding the deer hair forward after tying it on at the rear of the hook shank. Spiral wrap the working thread around the body to the head of the fly to secure the deer hair body in place.

At the head of the fly, clip off the excess deer hair and then tie in a second bundle of deer hair with the tips pointing forward as shown.

Between the body and the forward point bundle of deer hair, tie in a hackle of any color desired. Wrap the hackle around the hook shank as shown here, then tie off and clip the excess hackle.

Fold the forward bundle of deer hair back over the body of the hopper as shown so that the hackle extends only below the fly as small legs on the hopper. Tie it down with the working thread as shown.

Continue to make a wrap with the thread to make a collar and then tie off with a whip finish.

Deer Hair Hopper

This is a simple fly, tied with a body of wrapped deer hair. It is effective.

Hook: 2X to 4X long shank hook, sizes 10 to 2
Thread: yellow or tan, or to match material colors of hopper
Body: Deer body hair, in yellow, tan, green, or brown
Hackle (legs): Brown or black hackle
Hopper Legs: Molded T.N.T Hopper Legs
Tying instructions: Tie in the thread at mid-shank, then tie in, by the tip ends, a bundle of prepared deer hair pointing towards the rear. Fold the body hair forward. Carefully—to avoid spinning the deer hair around the hook shank—spiral-wrap the thread over this body until about ⅓ in back of the hook eye. Clip off excess deer hair. Tie down a separate bundle of deer hair, pointing forwards, keeping this bundle mostly on top of the hook shank. Wrap to the hook eye. Tie in a hackle and wrap it around the forward bundle to prepare legs. Tie off and clip excess. Return thread to the position about ⅓ in back of the hook eye. Fold the forward deer hair bundle back over the body and hook shank and tie down with the thread. Tie in a T.N.T. Hopper leg on each side and tie off with a whip finish.

Variations:

A better but more time-consuming way to make the segmented body is to spiral wrap the thread forward one segment length, then fold the body hair forward and tie down the segment with two thread wraps. Gently lift the body hair, make more spiral wraps for the next segment, and tie down again. Continue this way to the front of the body. This prevents the possibility of the body hair twisting on the hook shank as can occur with a basic spiral wrap of thread.

Add a short tail of red yarn if desired.

Tie in any color desired for season and your geographic area.

Example of grasshopper with the knotted feather legs
being tied in place.

Foam Hopper

Foam hoppers are legion since the first soft, closed cell foams were introduced years ago and tiers began experimenting with the material for flies. This hopper can be made by using foam cylinders, cut sections of foam, or formed and shaped bodies.

It is an easy tie, and one that can float forever. It can be tied in any color—light green for early season hoppers, brown or mottled brown for fall hoppers and in any size.

To tie a simple floating foam hopper, first tie on a hackle as shown at the rear of the hook shank.

Wrap the thread forward and then wrap the hackle forward, palmering it along the hook shank.

Weave the thread back through the hackle to the rear of the hook shank and then tie down and secure with a forward spiral. Wrap a foam body as shown here.

Clip the excess foam and then tie in a turkey feather section as shown.

Complete the fly by adding legs—either folded and knotted feather legs or T.N.T. hopper legs as shown here.

Hook: 2X long shank hook, sizes 14 to 6

Thread: Yellow, green, tan, or brown, depending upon color of hopper

Body: Foam cylinder or cut and trimmed foam sheeting in yellow, green, tan, or brown

Legs: Spiral palmer wrap of ginger or brown hackle

Hind Legs: Knotted hopper legs of yellow dyed or natural pheasant or turkey feather (Rainy Riding) or T.N.T. Hopper legs

Wing: Yellow, green, or tan dyed wing quill or mottled turkey feather

Tying instructions: Tie in the thread at the rear of the hook shank, then tie down a hackle by the tip. Wrap the thread forward to the hook eye, followed by the palmered hackle. Tie off and then weave the thread back through the hackle to the rear of the hook shank. At this point, tie down a shaped and sized body of sheet foam, molded foam, or a foam cylinder. The body can be cut by hand or with body shaper punches. The body should be the length of the hook shank or only slightly longer. If desired, add a little epoxy or cyanoacrylate glue to the shank side of the foam body to help stabilize it and keep it from rotating while fishing. Loosely spiral wrap up the hook shank to make slight (not tight) segments until about ⅓ in back of the hook eye. (Make sure to not matt the hackle legs.) Securely tie down the body with several wraps of thread at the ⅓ shank juncture. Prepare and tie down a wing of the same length as the body. Clip the excess wing flush with the head of the foam body, about the location of the hook eye. Finally, on each side tie in rear "hopper" legs and secure with several wraps. Complete with a whip finish.

Variations:

Tie in colors and sizes appropriate for your water, fishing season, and time of year.

A small variation of this in light green and tied thinly with a skinny body also serves well as a leafhopper imitation, with best sizes 16 through 12.

For a fuller body style, add a hackle to the fly after completing the above steps, and then wrap the hackle around the body—at the junction of the forward tie and tie-down position of the hopper legs.

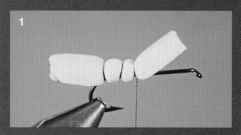

One simple way to tie a grasshopper-like fly is with a variation of a design by Bill Skilton. This involves first tying down and segmenting a shaped foam body as shown here.

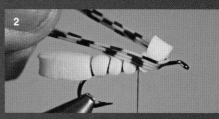

Bill runs legs of rubber through the foam body, but a simpler way is to loop the mottled legs around the body and above the hook shank as shown here.

Use the thread to wrap over the body and the legs at the same time, to hold them in place and angled towards the rear in this imitation.

Finish the fly by spiral wrapping the thread forward to secure the head of the foam to the hook shank

Example of the complete hopper fly, top view.

To tie a simple cricket, use a sheet of foam or a shaped body such as this Rainy Riding Gorilla body. Tie in a hackle as above and then tie down the foam body as shown.

Add a black or dark brown wing as shown here.

Complete the fly by adding hind legs of knotted feather or T.N.T. legs. Here, knotted legs are used for this cricket.

Top view of the above simple foam cricket.

Foam Cricket

This is a simple foam variation of the above foam cricket and tied the same way, except for using black materials. The best materials are as follows:

Hook: 2X long, sizes 14 to 6
Thread: Black
Body: Black foam sheeting, cut into strip and tied down
Legs: Black palmered hackle
Hind Legs: Black synthetic hopper legs or black feather section, tied with overhand knot
Wing: Black feather section or section of wing quill
Tying instructions: Tie just as the foam hopper above is tied.

Variations:

No variations.

Gorilla Foam Hopper

This fly is tied exactly as the foam hopper previously mentioned, with the exception of using Rainy Riding Gorilla Foam Bodies in four or five segments, as you prefer, based on the size of the fly. The segments in the foam body make for natural places to spiral wrap a fly, or to run the thread around the hook to make two or three turns of thread around the foam between each pair of segments. As with all hoppers, this can be tied in all colors. Because of the size of the Gorilla foam bodies, it is best in sizes 8 through 4 for the five-segment bodies; 10 through 6 for the four-segment style.

Hook: Hooks 2X long, sizes 12 to 2
Thread: Yellow, or to match the color of the hopper being tied
Tail: Short length of turkey feather
Body: Gorilla foam in yellow or color desired
Wing: Section of turkey feather
Collar: Deer or antelope hair, yellow, or dyed to color of hopper
Hopper Legs: Rainy Riding knotted turkey or pheasant hopper legs or T.N.T. Hopper legs
Tying instructions: Tie in at the middle of the hook. Then wrap the thread back to the rear. Tie in tail of turkey feather. Position a Gorilla body (four segments for flies in sizes 6 and smaller; five segments in sizes 8 and larger. Tie two thread wraps around the rear of the foam body, then wrap the thread around the hook shank several turns while holding the foam up and out of the way. Make two more wraps around the body and continue this way to make segments up to close to the hook eye. Tied properly, the head will angle up and slightly forward of the hook shank. Tie in a prepared section of turkey feather, then overwrap with a small, prepared bundle of deer hair. Trim the deer hair ahead of the wrap and make several more wraps to secure it. Tie in hopper legs—one on each side of the body—and complete the fly with a whip finish.

To tie a simple hopper, tie in a tail of turkey or similar mottled feather and wrap forward and back. Then, tie in a shaped, Gorilla foam body and segment forward.

Next, add a turkey wing as shown, tying flat or upright as desired.

Add a bundle of deer hair and tie off securely.

Tie in legs to complete the fly. In this case, knotted feather legs simulate the hind hopper legs.

An example of the lengths to which different materials can be used. This is a cricket with a furled body made of black deer hair and finished with a wing and head of black deer hair.

Examples of simple crickets tied with furled deer hair body (left) and simple foam and wing pattern (right).

A similar use of materials in black will create this black cricket.

Gorilla Foam Cricket

This is tied just as is the Gorilla Foam Hopper above, using black four- or five-segment bodies based on the size of the hook. It is a great looking, high floating cricket.

Hook: Hooks 2X long, sizes 12 to 2
Thread: Black
Tail: Short length of black dyed turkey feather or black section of quill
Body: Black Gorilla foam
Wing: Section of turkey feather, dyed black or black quill section
Collar: Deer or antelope hair, dyed black
Hopper Legs: Knotted turkey feather or Rainy Riding knotted pheasant hopper legs in black or colored black with felt tip pens
Tying instructions: Tie in exactly as with the Gorilla Foam Hopper above, only using black materials as indicated here.

Variations:
No variations.

Bullethead Hopper

Bullethead hoppers are a basic variation of the Keith Fulsher bullet head Thunder Creek flies which in turn are a variation of an old Carrie Stevens (famous Maine tier of the Ghost series of flies fame) design. They are made by tying down a bundle of bucktail with the tips forward and then pulling the hair back to wrap in a "neck" area to make for a smooth, round bullet head. The use of deer hair makes this ideal for hopper imitations that can be tied several ways, as per the variations. This hopper floats low in the water—most real hoppers do—with only the deer hair for flotation.

Hook: 2X long shank hooks, sizes 12 to 4
Thread: Yellow, tan, or brown, depending upon deer hair and fly color desired
Tail: Section of yellow wing quill
Body: Yellow, tan, or brown yarn
Legs (Palmered hackle): Ginger or brown hackle, palmered over the body
Wing: Section of turkey quill
Head: Yellow, tan, or brown deer hair, tied bullethead style
Collar: Tips of deer hair from the bullet head

You can tie simple or complex bullethead hoppers. This starts with a tail of yellow wing quill as shown.

Continue by tying in a hackle to be palmered forward later in the tying process.

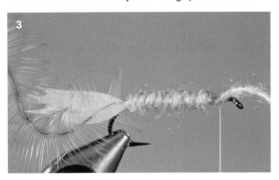

Tie in a body material of stranded synthetic dubbing to work up and down the shank as a body for the hopper.

Wrap the body material up and down the hook shank and tie off at the head of the hook as shown.

Add a turkey feather for a wing as shown. The next step adds a deer-hair bundle with tips pointed forward.

Make sure that the thread is back to where you tied on the wing before continuing.

Pull the deer-hair bundle back over the wing and around the body, then tie the bundle down with a light wrap partway back from the hook eye and head.

Tying instructions: Tie in at the midpoint of the hook, wrap to the rear and tie down the yellow wing quill section for the tail. Tie in the palmered hackle by the tip. Return to the midpoint of the hook, tie in yellow, tan, or brown yarn and wrap the thread forward to a little in back of the hook eye. Wrap the yarn up and down the hook shank to form the body. Do not make the body too thick, since you will be overlaying this with the reversed deer hair. Palmer the hackle over the body to form legs. Tie in a section of turkey feather for the wing. Prepare a bundle (remove underfur) of deer hair and trim to the right length. This length should be about twice the length of the hook shank. Tie down in back of the hook eye with the tips pointing forward. Wrap back over the butt of deer hair and the wing to a point about ¼ to ⅓ back of the hook eye. Fold the deer hair back over the tie-down point so that the tips are now uniformly veiling the body and pointed towards the rear. Use the thread at the ¼ to ⅓ hook shank length to wrap over the deer hair to secure this bullet head and the collar. Make sure that the overlapping bundle of deer hair is positioned evenly around the hook shank. Tie off with a whip finish. Seal with head cement.

Variations:

As suggested, tie in any color yarn and deer hair to simulate the hoppers in your area. Use stranding body material such as Gudebrod E-Z Dub, Rainy Riding S-T-R-E-T-C-H Flex, mohair, or floss.

Use a tied-down foam cylinder or cut section of sheet foam for the body in place of the yarn or other materials for more flotation, longer flotation, and higher floating in rough riffle waters.

Tie with a yarn body and in place of the palmered hackle, tie in a hackle wrap in front of the body and before adding the wing and bullet head material of deer hair. Fold the deer hair over the top of the body so that the hackle sticks out ventrally to simulate legs.

Bullethead Cricket

This fly is tied exactly as above and with the same variations, with the exception that all the materials are black. Thus, this bullethead cricket has a black quill tail, black yarn body, black palmered hackle legs, black feather wing, and head/collar of black deer hair. As with the hopper variations, it can be tied using other stranded body materials such as E-Z Dub, stretch materials, floss, etc. It can also be tied with a black foam body as per a variation of the bullethead hopper. These also can be tied with brown materials to simulate mole or camel crickets. Note, however, that these are less common than the common black crickets found everywhere.

While the Muddler Minnow originated in 1950 by Don Gapen and was designed to imitate bottom-living sculpins, it also works as a hopper imitation when tied unweighted and dressed with fly floatant. In the original dressing, the gold tinsel body might be a little much for a hopper, but the deer hair collar and head and the turkey feather wing make it a good hopper imitation anyway. Variations can make this into an even more life-like hopper imitation. The original was tied with a weighted body to get deep where sculpins live, but this is left out of this floating hopper design.

Hook: 2X to 4X long hooks, sizes 12 to 2
Thread: Brown
Tail: Mottled turkey quill fibers
UnderBody: White or gold floss to build up body to cigar shape, to be covered with body material
Body: Oval or flat gold tinsel (Mylar can be used)
Underwing: Gray squirrel tail
Overwing: Mottled turkey quill section
Collar: Brown deer hair, spun
Head: Trimmed and clipped butt ends of spun brown deer hair

The Muddler Minnow, when tied unweighted, is an ideal imitation of a grasshopper. To tie this, begin as here by tying on a tail of turkey feather.

Continue tying by building up a cigar-shaped body of yarn or floss.

Return to the rear of the fly and tie in a tinsel or Mylar wrap, then wrap the thread forward followed by the tinsel as shown here.

Tie in the two-part wing of squirrel tail and turkey feather.

Complete the fly by tying down a bundle of deer hair with the tips to the rear and clip the front to a round head or collar.

Tying instructions: Tie down the thread at the midpoint of the hook shank and wrap to the rear. Tie in the tail of turkey quill, then the gold tinsel or Mylar, followed by tying down floss. Wrap the thread forward to slightly in back of the hook eye. Wrap the floss forward to make a smooth cigar-shaped body, then tie off. Follow with an even wrap of tinsel or Mylar and tie off at the head of the fly. Tie down an underwing of gray squirrel, followed by a tie-down of turkey quill. Clip excess. Tie in a bundle of prepared (under-fur removed) deer hair with the tips to the rear. Clip the butt ends to form a round or tapered head, and tie off with a whip finish.

Variations:

Tie in any color desired, such as yellow, light green, tan, or dark brown.

Substitute tan, yellow, light green yarn for the body.

Substitute yellow, light green, or tan thin foam for the standard gold body.

Parachute hoppers and crickets: In many cases, you will not need hackle or parachute hackle for hoppers or crickets, particularly if you have a foam body or deer hair head or wings. One way that I like to use parachute hackle for these terrestrials is to turn the fly over in the vise and tie the post and wrapped hackle on the underside of the fly where the hackle can more closely simulate the smaller forward legs of a hopper. If you wish to add the larger "jumping" legs, these can be tied in separately using knotted hackle stems, knotted rubber legs, knotted pheasant, or turkey feather fibers, T.N.T. Hopper Legs, or similar materials.

One easy way to tie a hopper is to use thick macramé cord and furl it as shown, then tie to a hook shank. Regular length hooks can be used for this hopper tie.

Finish the fly by adding a wing of bundled deer hair in natural brown or tan color as shown. Clip the front butt bundle as you would for a Muddler Minnow.

Tying a simple grasshopper: First tie in a length of body material—in this case a length of EZ-Dub from Gudebrod.

Wrap the thread forward followed by the body material and then tie in a turkey feather for a wing.

Add knotted feather legs as shown and tie down on both sides.

Add a hackle to form legs.

Clip any excess hackle.

Wrap the hackle as shown to form a head and legs to the grasshopper.

SINKING HOPPERS, CRICKETS

Stranded Dubbing Hopper

Yarn, E-Z Dub, mohair, etc. makes a good body material for sinking flies. The main difference between these and similar body material floating hoppers is that the floating hoppers use deer hair as a floating material for a fly that floats in the surface film. These sinking styles use webby wet fly hackle for a wrap around the head of the fly to simulate legs, antennae and the bulk of a head.

Hook: 2X long shank hook, sizes 12 to 4

Thread: Yellow, tan, green or brown, depending upon color of hopper tied

Body: Stranded material such as yarn, E-Z Dub, or similar materials

Wing: Dyed feathers to match the hopper or a mottled turkey quill section

Hackle: Webby wet-fly ginger or brown

Legs: Rainy Riding Knotted Hopper Legs

Tying instructions: Tie in the thread at mid-shank, then tie in the body material. Wrap the thread forward to a point ⅓ in back of the hook eye. Wrap the body material up and down the shank to form a neat tapered body and tie off at the thread position. Add a feather wing, then tie down a pair of knotted hopper legs. Tie in a hackle and wrap around the head. Clip the excess and tie off with a whip finish.

Variations:

Tie in different colors, based on the season and color of hoppers near your waters.

Vary the stranded material as desired.

Stranded Dubbing Cricket

This cricket it made the same way as the stranded dubbing hopper, except all black materials are used. If knotted hopper legs are not available in black, a quick solution is to use a felt tip marker to color standard knotted legs. You can also use rubber legs. Make sure that you use webby hackle so that the fly sinks. Tie in brown if you wish to simulate a mole or camel cricket.

To tie a grasshopper terrestrial with a furled body, first tie down one or two strands of yarn as shown. If the yarn is not thick and you wish a thicker body, use two strands as shown here.

Hold the two strands after tying them down and twist as shown in the direction of the manufacturer's twist to furl the yarn.

This is just a different way to tie hoppers using a furled body instead of one that is wrapped around the hook shank. Thus, a regular length hook is used for these.

Hook: Standard length hooks, sizes 12 to 4

Thread: Yellow, green, tan, or brown, depending upon hopper color desired.
Body: Furled yarn or stranded material in yellow, cream, light green, tan, or brown
Wing: Yellow, cream, light green, tan feather or mottled turkey feather quill section
Hackle: Webby wet fly hackle, ginger or brown
Legs: Hopper legs in color to match hopper
Tying instructions: Tie in the thread at a point ⅓ back from the hook eye. Tie down the body material. Twist one end of the body material, in the same direction that it was made, to furl it. When twisted, fold it over and tie down. This material twists on itself. The length of this furled body should be about 1½ to 2 times the length of the hook shank. Tie in a feather wing section and then a pair of hopper legs. Tie down a hackle and wrap it forward and back between the tie down point and the hook eye. Complete using a whip finish.

Variations:
Tie in any color desired

Furled Cricket. Tie a furled cricket just as you do a furled hopper, above, but use all black materials for the body, hackle, wings, and legs.

Chenille Hopper
Sinking chenille hoppers are nothing more than one-wrap bulky bodies (the chenille) that result in hoppers very similar to previous yarn hopper designs. They are easy to tie and sink well as the hopper body soaks up water.

Fold the yarn over the twist on itself, and then tie down in the spot where the yarn was tied originally.

Add a turkey feather for a wing as shown and tie off. Extra materials can be added if you like, including a hackle for legs and rear hopper legs.

Hook: 2X long shank hook in sizes 12 to 6

Thread: To match hopper desired—yellow, green, tan and brown

Body: Yellow, green, tan, or brown chenille

Wing: Wings to match body color; of dyed feathers or mottled turkey quill

Hackle: Webby wet-fly; brown or ginger

Legs: Knotted hopper legs

Tying instructions: Tie the same way (above) as with a yarn or furled body hopper.

Variations:

Use any color materials to make different color hoppers.

For a variation, tie in the hackle at the rear of the fly, then tie and wrap the body, followed by palmering the hackle up the body before tying down the feather wing and hopper legs. This is just a variation of how the legs look on the completed fly.

chapter

Cicada Killer. Cicada killers are just what the name indicates—they catch and kill cicadas. As you might expect, these are large insects, looking like bees on steroids or possibly a Chernobyl bee. They are about 1½ inches long, with wings longer than one inch. The rear of the abdomen is dark (black) with the forward part banded yellow and black, as are bees. They are big and impressive insects. They catch and paralyze cicadas as food for their young after capturing them on the wing and paralyzing them. These insects dig individual burrows in the dirt, with most of their burrows at an angle, with the dirt from the digging piled up at the entrance to the hole. Eggs are deposited into the hole, along with a paralyzed cicada to provide food for the growing young. Some big cicadas require dragging to the burrow rather than flying them there. I cannot figure out how to do it—or guarantee it would work better than a basic cicada or cicada killer imitation—but an imitation that would incorporate both killer and cicada would be a copy of a real-life scenario that might work well on the water for larger fish.

Foam Cicada Killer

Hook: 2X long shank hook, sizes 4 to 1. For a curved body as they often are when dying, tie on a Mustad 37160 hook or similar curved shank hook.

Thread: Black

Body: Yellow and black banded foam

Wings: Transparent or silver wing materials, tied in a back angled and splayed fashion at the thorax

Thorax: Black or black-colored foam

Head: Black foam

Legs: Dark brown hackle

Antennae: Black hackle stems

To tie a cicada killer from a striped foam cylinder, first cut partway through the body with a razor blade so that the body will fit onto the hook shank. Taper the rear end of the foam cylinder with flame and rolling the body between your fingers, or by sanding, to make it tapered and rounded.

Tie thread on the hook and then add CA or similar glue to the hook shank and seat the foam body in place. Add several wraps in one place around the front part of the cylinder. Note that this body should be no more than ⅔ of the length of the hook shank so that there is room for the rest of the materials.

In front of the foam cylinder, tie in a hackle to make the legs of the imitation.

Tie in a strip of black foam with foam pointed towards the front of the fly. Wrap the thread slightly forward and then back before wrapping the hackle in place.

Wrap the hackle around the hook shank and tie off, then clip the remainder of the hackle.

Fold the foam over and tie down, then clip off the excess foam from the fly.

Add a wing of flash material or sheet material and tie off to complete the fly. This fly is shown with a life-size (1½ inch-long body) cicada killer for size comparison.

Tying instructions: Tie in the working thread at the center of the hook shank and tie down a length of black/yellow banded foam. You can buy such foam in banded colors or make your own using yellow foam marked with a black felt tip marker. Wrap the thread back up to just forward of the center of the hook shank, fold over the foam and tie down. Tie in the wings, one on each side and angled back and out. Tie in the hackle. Wrap the thread forward. Tie in a length (strip) of black sheet foam, pointed forward, to form the head and thorax. Follow this with the hackle, tied off in back of the hook eye. Wrap the thread back slightly, weaving in between the hackle. Fold the foam over and tie down to form a head. Hold the foam up and out of the way and continue to wrap over the hook shank with the thread until reaching the body. Fold down the foam and tie off, with any short remaining foam folded over the butt end of the wings. Tie off with a whip finish.

Variations:

Tie the entire fly with one length of black/yellow foam, using a black felt tip marker to color the head and thorax black. For this, tie in sections progressing forward, tying down the wings at the junction of the thorax and abdomen. It is almost like tying a Chernobyl ant except with wings tied in between the thorax and head.

Floating Foam Bee

A floating foam bee is similar to the cicada killer above, although much smaller in size. The materials and steps for this are similar and as follows:

Hook: Regular length hook, sizes 14 through 6

Thread: Black

To begin a simple bee, mark a strip of yellow foam with black felt tip marker to make bands as shown and then tie down at the rear of the fly with the bands down. When the strip of foam is folded over, the bands of color will be on top.

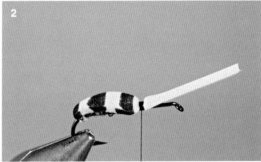

Continue tying a foam bee by folding the foam over the hook shank and tying down as shown, about ⅓ in back of the hook eye. Note that the bands of felt tip marker color (black on yellow foam) now show.

Tie in wings of clear sheet material. These wing materials are available in all fly tying shops.

As above, showing the crinkled clear sheet material used for wings in many flies.

Make a slight waist and tie in a clipped black hackle to serve as legs. Note that the forward part of the foam has been clipped off, leaving enough to form a head.

Completed fly with the hackle, wings, and head.

Heads on bees are not yellow in most cases, so this yellow head on this imitation is colored black using a felt tip permanent marker.

Body: Black and yellow foam sheet strip, or yellow foam banded with black felt tip marker

Thorax/Head: Foam colored black with black felt tip marker

Wings: Transparent or silver wing material

Legs: Brown or black hackle

Tying instructions: Tie in the thread in the middle of the hook shank, tie down a length of foam strip or cylinder, and wrap to the rear. Wrap the thread back up to the ⅔ mark in back of the eye, fold over the foam and tie down. At this point, tie in wings one on each side, angled and flared, and then tie in a hackle. Wrap the hackle around the body at this point and tie off, then complete the fly with a whip finish. Finish by coloring the head black with a black felt tip marker.

Variations:

Tie in any size and in other similar colors. Possibilities would be white and black, orange and black, yellow and brown, orange and brown.

Floating Foam Wasp. Tie wasps similarly to bees, but on a longer shank hook and in a larger size. Most wasps are larger and longer than bees so hooks in the 2X to 4X length, sizes 6 to 2, are best. Tie with the same colors and techniques as above for the bee.

Floating Foam Hornet. I generally think of hornets as being mostly, or all, black or dark brown, while wasps are black and yellow, as are bees. That is not completely true, although it seems to be the case where I live and fish. My "hornets" are patterns that are tied basically with the same materials and steps as with a wasp or bee (above) but with an all-black or all-brown body in place of the variegated or banded yellow/black foam body. Best sizes are the same as those for wasps—2X to 4X long, about size 6 to 2.

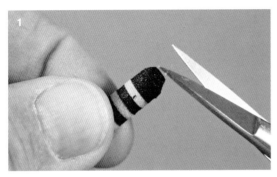

Another way to tie a bee is to use scissors to lightly trim the rear end of the foam body to make it tapered and life-like.

To tie a bee that is not abnormally fat, use a razor blade to cut the foam cylinder in half lengthwise.

Hold the half-foam body over the hook shank and tie down in the middle with the thread, just as you would when tying a foam McMurray ant pattern.

Tie in flash wing material (sheet material can also be used). Tie the flash down at an angle and then fold it over and tie again so that you have two wings aimed towards the rear of the bee.

Top view of bee pattern.

Angled view. This is a different bee, as it has "legs" of a wrap or two of cactus chenille.

Side view of bee with cactus chenille for legs.

The last step on any foam bee is to tie down the foam head as shown to complete it and give the fly a realistic rounded head.

An easy way to tie bees is to use the prepared bee bodies that are similar to balsa McMurray ant bodies and available from Rod Yerger. Tie in the middle by the mono waist.

To finish a McMurray-style bee, tie in a clipped hackle as shown here.

Completed McMurray-style bee.

SINKING BEES, WASPS, HORNETS

McGinty

This might be considered one of the first or at least an early bee pattern with the alternate bands of black and yellow chenille. It is and always has been a sinking fly, and ideal for panfish and bluegill. It is also good for trout and other species, but panfish seem to be particularly attracted to the right colors of this fly.

Hook: Regular hook, sizes 12 to 8
Thread: Brown
Tail: Mixed red-dyed hackle fibers and barred teal flank feathers
Body: Alternate bands of black and yellow chenille
Wings: White-tipped mallard secondary wing quill sections
Hackle: Brown
Weight (Optional): Strips or a short wrap or lead wire for weight and fast sinking
Tying instructions: Tie in the thread in the center of the hook shank and wrap to the bend of the hook, wrapping down the mixed teal and red hackle fibers for the tail. Tie in the black and yellow strands of chenille. Wrap the thread forward followed by the spiral bands of yellow and black chenille. Tie off both behind the hook eye, leaving enough room for the hackle and wings. Tie in a throat or collar hackle, wrapping the collar hackle, if used, and tying off. Prepare the wings of mallard and tie in place over the collar hackle. Clip the excess and tie off, then complete the fly with a whip finish.

To tie an underwater bee pattern such as a McGinty, tie in a tail of red hackle and barred teal along with a strand each of black and yellow chenille.

Wrap the thread and then the two strands of chenille forward to make the alternate bands of the bee body.

Tie in a hackle to make the legs.

The McGinty, with the hackle tied in place but the wings still to be added.

The completed McGinty with the wings of white tipped mallard or similar feather tied in place, wet fly style.

Variations:

Tie with an initial wrap or placement of lead or non-lead strips for weight and to aid sinking of the fly. No other variations are suggested, since this would change the fly from the basic McGinty pattern.

Sinking Chenille Bee

This is a simple version of the McGinty, and used the same way. As with the McGinty, it is a prime pattern for bluegills, or other panfish and sunfish, when they are on the beds.

Hook: Standard hook, sizes 12 to 6
Thread: Black
Body: Bands made with two strands of black and yellow chenille
Hackle: Brown or ginger
Wings: Section of white wing quill
Weight (Optional): Lead or non-lead wire, wrapped or laid parallel to hook shank and wrapped in place
Tying instructions: As above, first tie in the thread and then wrap down any lead or non-lead wire used to rapidly sink the fly. Wrap the thread to the rear and tie in the black and yellow strands of chenille. Wrap the thread forward to behind the hook eye, leaving room

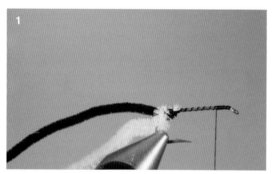

To tie a simple sinking-style bee, tie in, at the rear of the hook, a strand each of yellow and black chenille as shown.

Wrap the thread forward and then follow with the two strands of chenille. These two strands can be wrapped together, or one spiraled up, followed between the spirals by the other. Tie off as shown.

Clip the excess and tie a base on which to tie in the wings.

Tie in wings of flash or sheet material to simulate the clear wings of a bee. These are of a few strands of flash material.

Top view, showing the flash wings tied in place.

The next step is to tie in a hackle to make the legs of the bee. Either ginger or black hackle can be used.

Wrap the hackle around the shank of the hook to complete the hackle and to complete the bee.

for the hackle and wing. Follow with the two strands of chenille, for making black and yellow bands around the hook shank. Tie off and clip excess. Tie in the hackle and wrap around the hook shank, then tie off and clip. Add the wings, clip the excess and complete the fly with a whip finish.

Variations:

As mentioned above, this fly can be tied with or without the lead/non-lead wire for weight.

Other colors can be used, still keeping the barred appearance. Options are black and white, black and orange, and brown and yellow.

Sinking Yarn Bee. Tie this pattern the same way as the above bee, just using black and yellow yarn for the body in place of the chenille. As with the above bee, you can tie without weight or add lead or non-lead wire for faster sinking. A variation of this is to use stranded material other than yarn for the body. Examples would be Gudebrod E-Z Dub or similar colored materials.

Sinking Chenille, Yarn, or E-Z Dub Hornet or Wasp. These are nothing more than larger sizes of the bee listed above. They may be tied in any size and with any material using the basic black and yellow or other color combinations. Other options are to tie unweighted, or with lead or non-lead wire for weight and faster sinking. Best hooks for these are 2X to 4X long hooks in sizes 6 to 2. Use the same materials as listed above for the bee patterns and follow the same basic directions for tying.

Sinking Cicada Killer

These giant wasp-like creatures (they are true wasps, but larger than normal wasps) are a big meal for most fish. They are too big to be taken in by panfish and bluegills, not that some of them won't try. One slight change from other wasp patterns is with the black rear of the body, which is typical of these insects that capture and paralyze cicadas to store as food for their young.

Hook: 2X long shank hook, sizes 4 to 1
Thread: Black
Abdomen: Black and yellow bands of chenille
Thorax: Black chenille
Head: Black Chenille
Wings: Clear Super Hair, Ultra Hair, or similar gossamer wing material
Legs (Hackle): Black or brown hackle
Tying instructions: Tie in the thread at the midpoint on the hook, then wrap to the rear and tie in black chenille. Wrap the thread forward about ⅓ the shank length and tie in yellow chenille. Wrap forward to a point about ⅔ up the hook shank. Wrap the black chenille around the hook shank up to the thread position, then wrap back to the yellow chenille tie-down spot to build up the body. Wrap forward again with both the black and yellow chenille to make a banded abdomen and tie off. Clip excess yellow chenille. Tie in hackle and wrap around the hook shank to create the appearance of legs. Tie down the wings, with the wings flat back or flared out as preferred. Continue to tie forward with the black chenille, then back to the thread to tie off to form the head and thorax. Complete with a whip finish.

Variations:

Tie with lead or non-lead wire wrap or parallel strands of wire for added weight and sinking.

7 chapter

You will not really find a hatch of inchworms. In spring and early summer you can find an abundance of them along stream-side trees and bushes. When they fall into the water, they create a food source for any trout or panfish looking for an easy meal. There are a lot of patterns for inchworms, and they can be tied of deer hair, foam, chenille, Ultra Chenille, yarn, floss, even electricians tape. One popular imitation in the East and Mid-Atlantic area is the Green Weenie, a simple chenille imitation that, depending upon how it is tied, can also imitate a caddis nymph or small caterpillar. Different anglers have different views as to what the pattern imitates. Note that inchworms have legs only at each end, unlike most caterpillars that have legs along the full length of their body. Thus, they arch their body when they walk. Inchworm imitations include:

Green Weenie

There are variations of this, depending upon whether you are tying simple or more time-consuming versions. Even the most complicated version is simple

Hook: Size 8 or 10 2X or 3X long shank hook
Thread: Light green
Body: Light green or chartreuse chenille
Head: None, or wrap of peacock herl
Tying instructions: Tie in the thread and then the chenille at the rear of the hook shank. Make a short fold-over loop tail of the chenille and tie down at the hook bend. Wrap the thread up the shank, followed by the wrap of chenille. Tie off and clip the chenille a short length in back of the hook eye. Tie in several strands of peacock herl, and wrap to the hook eye and back. Tie off and clip the herl. Complete the fly with a whip finish.

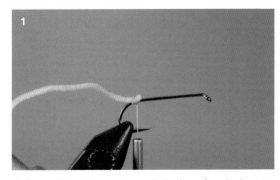

A Green Weenie can be an imitation of an inchworm or a caddis larva, depending upon how it is finished. To tie this, start by tying in a strand of chenille or Ultra Chenille at the rear of the hook as shown.

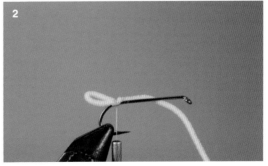

Double over the strand of chenille as shown to make a loop and tie down again.

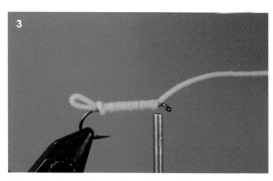

Wrap the thread forward and then follow with the chenille wrapped around the hook. Tie off.

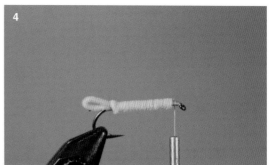

Clip the excess to complete the fly and tie off when complete with a whip finish. Some tiers like to include a head of peacock herl.

To tie a straight inchworm, tie down the chenille at the rear of the hook shank as shown. Use the same color thread as the inchworm.

Spiral over the hook shank and chenille as you work up to the eye of the hook.

Tie off at the eye of the hook and then clip the inchworm chenille to length—usually a little longer than the hook shank.

Variations:

Tie without the head of peacock herl. This head of peacock herl makes it more a caddis nymph imitation than an inchworm variation anyway.

After tying down the chenille to the hook, omit the loop of chenille for the tail and just tie the light green chenille up the hook shank. This can be tied with or without the peacock herl head.

Tie inchworms in different colors. You can never underestimate the strange taste of fish.

Walking Inchworm

These are tied like a red manure or San Juan worm using Vernille or Ultra Chenille. The main difference is that the chenille is tied only at both ends of the hook shank and allowed to "arch" above the hook shank. As a walking inchworm on a hook, it resembles an inchworm walking on a short twig.

Hook: Size 8 or 10 2X long hook
Thread: Black (so as to not make a wrapped green hook shank when wrapping to the head of the fly)
Body: Light green or chartreuse Vernille or Ultra Chenille

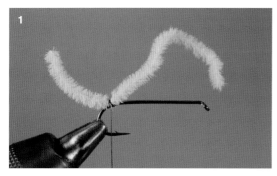

To tie a walking inchworm, tie in a length of chenille at the rear of the hook, using black thread. The black thread allows wrapping over the hook shank without the thread detracting from the chenille worm.

Wrap the thread forward around the hook shank.

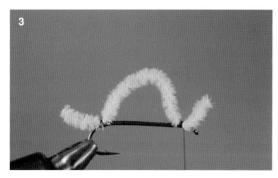

Tie down the chenille again with the thread, making an arch in the chenille to make it appear like an inchworm walking on a twig.

Tying instructions: Prepare the chenille by flaming and rolling the ends between your fingers to taper it. Use material about two times the length of the hook shank. Tie in the thread at the rear of the hook shank, then tie in the chenille, leaving a very short "tail," which simulates the walking legs of the inchworm. Wrap the thread forward to the eye of the hook, then tie off the other end of the chenille, leaving an arch of chenille and a small tag end of chenille extending in front of the hook eye.

Variations:

You can also tie this with yarn or dubbing, furling the strand of body material to twist it, then tying down at the rear and again tying at the front of the hook to make an arched inchworm.

Foam Inchworm

There are several ways to tie foam inchworms, including those tied directly to the hook, those with an extended body, and those arching above the hook, as with a walking-style inchworm. The following is for a simple foam inchworm tied to a hook shank.

Hook: Long shank, about 4X in length, hook sizes 10 and 12

Thread: Green

Body: Light green foam cylinder or thin strip cut from sheet foam. Use very thin foam strips.

Tying instructions: Tie in the thread at the rear of the hook, then tie down a length of light green foam in thin (⅛ inch) cylinder form, or a strip of sheet foam cut into a 1/16 or ⅛ inch-wide strip. Segment the body by spiraling over it as you wrap up the shank, or wrap a few turns over the hook shank between wraps over the hook and foam. Tie off in back of the hook eye, then trim the remainder of the foam to extend slightly in front of the hook eye.

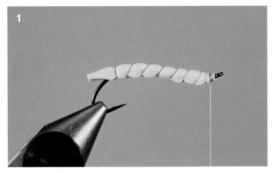

To tie a foam or floating inchworm, cut a thin strip of foam in a light green color and tie down to the hook shank. Make sure that the foam wraps around the hook shank, and use the same color thread as the foam as you spiral wrap the thread up the hook to tie off.

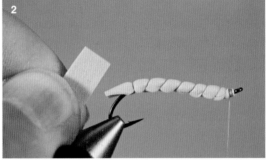

Example of finished foam inchworm and the sheet foam strip used to tie it.

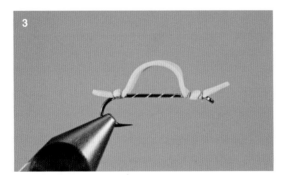

Floating inchworms can be tied out of foam as shown here. The secret is to use a few thin strips of foam and tie down along the length of the hook, or at the two ends, as shown here, for a walking inchworm.

Variations:

Use foam cylinder to make a walking inchworm by tying down at the rear, then spiraling the thread up the hook shank, arching the foam into an inverted "U" and tying down again in back of the hook eye.

To make an extended body inchworm, use a thin strip of light green foam about three times the length of the hook shank, and tie it in the middle with light green thread. Hold it in your fingers for this operation. Then fold the foam over itself at the tie-down point, clip the excess thread, and bring the thread between the two parallel strips of foam before wrapping over the two pieces of foam and continuing with the thread between the foam. After several such wraps to segment the body, hold the foam over the rear of the hook shank and tie it to the hook. Continue the same way, bringing the thread between the foam and even around the hook shank between the segment wraps over the foam and hook. When reaching the end, trim the foam and tie off or continue with wraps over the foam only for several segments forward of the hook eye.

Tie in the thread at the rear of the hook, then tie down a thin strip of foam. Wrap the thread forward to just in back of the hook eye and follow with a spiral wrap of the light green foam. Tie off, clip the excess foam, and complete the fly with a whip finish.

Hair Body Inchworm

Hair body inchworms can be tied in several ways. All body hair from deer and relatives is hollow, so that it floats, allowing the completed inchworm to float in the surface film, resembling a live inchworm. If possible, use thin hair, such as dyed antelope or caribou, rather than the thicker hair of deer. You may have to use deer, since this is dyed more typically in the colors (light green) necessary for such flies. Such flies from deer hair can be tied in bullet, bundled, and arched/walking methods.

Hook: 2X to 4X long shank hook, sizes 10 and 12
Thread: Light green
Body: Light green body hair

To tie a deer hair inchworm, first tie in a bundle of light green dyed deer hair as shown. Tie down either the tip or butt ends.

Use the thread to spiral wrap over the bundle of deer hair at the rear of the hook. To do this, hold the bundle and spiral wrap to the end of the bundle, then reverse the wrap back to the hook as shown.

Continue the wrap up the hook shank to the eye of the hook and then bend the deer hair bundle in an arch as shown and tie down to complete the walking inchworm appearance.

Clipped and completed deer hair bundle inchworm.

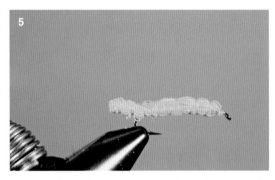

You can also tie inchworms with extended bodies. This is an example of an inchworm with an extended body made from a bundle of light green deer hair. This is made similar to the walking inchworm, using a bundle of deer hair. The tying is easier since the bundle is tied in place and spiral wrapped on the hook shank as shown.

Tying instructions: For a bundled-body inchworm, use a long shank hook (4X to 6X) and tie in the thread at the rear of the hook shank. Clip and prepare a bundle of body hair about the thickness of a large wood match. Tie this bundle down at the rear so that it extends beyond the eye of the hook. Make one or two wraps of thread, then make two spiral wraps around the hook shank only, followed by two wraps around the hook and body hair. Continue until reaching the eye of the hook. Tie off, and complete with a whip finish. Trim the body hair on both ends.

Variations:

Tie the body hair down on the rear of the hook shank, then spiral wrap up the hook shank and over the body hair, then reverse the wrap down the body and over the extended body protruding from the rear of the hook shank. This step takes care and a light touch, since you are wrapping over only the hair with no hook support. At the rear of the bundle, reverse this spiral wrap to the rear of the hook shank and tie off with a whip finish.

To vary the above, extend the body in front of the hook eye and make the wrap over this extended part, forward and back, just as you do with the rear bundle described above.

Arched Hair-Body Bullethead Inchworm

Hook: 2X to 4X long, size 12 or 10 hook

Thread: Light green

Body: Light green deer, antelope, or caribou hair

Tying instructions: Bullet-style inchworms were first developed by Poul Jorgensen using the tying technique of Carrie Stevens and later, Keith Fulsher (bullet head flies).

To make an arched/walking style of inchworm with body hair, prepare a bundle of hair, tie in the thread at the front of the hook. Leave a long tag end of thread and do not clip. Wrap the thread to the rear. Tie in the bundle of body hair with the main part of the bundle extending in back of the hook shank to the rear. Fold the hair bundle over itself and then tie down on the hook shank. Separate the bundle from the hook shank and wrap thread around the bundle only. Spiral wrap the thread up and down the hair bundle and tie off at the rear of the fly. Clip the excess thread. Bend the bundle of hair over the hook shank to make an inverted "U" arch. Hold the forward part of the bundle over the front of the hook shank and tie down and off with the tag end of thread. Complete with a whip finish.

See instructions in Chapter 2—Simple Tying Steps and Special Tricks—for a method of making easy wraps over a bundle of body hair by using a needle in a vise as a temporary support.

WORMS

Worms—the real ones, not the ones that we tie—are a fishing staple for lots of anglers. Many of us started fishing with spinning gear by drifting a worm through a trout riffle or soaking it in a farm pond. Worms have been described by their species, and various colloquial names such as earthworms, red worms, nightcrawlers, nightwalkers, manure worms, etc. Flies to imitate worms only came along with the San Juan worm tie that is designed to imitate the small red worms found in some streams and on which trout and other fish feed. It is not a terrestrial, even though an easy tie and one not unlike those for inchworms. This red manure worm is really the same tie.

Using red or burgundy Ultra Chenille with the ends tapered in flame, it is easy to tie manure worms by using red thread and tying the chenille along the length of the hook shank as shown.

You can tie worms that imitate larger worms for not only trout, but also for bass fishing and angling for panfish, crappie, perch, and other species that eat these wriggly, meaty morsels.

The possibilities range from simple worms in which a strand of Vernille or Ultra Chenille is tied to a hook, up through ties of doubled and twisted cactus chenille to make a large worm that is the fly fisherman's equivalent of the soft plastic worm tossed by the hardware guys. Most of these worms are tied in worm colors of red, brown, rust, pink, tan, maroon, and such, although you can tie worms in any color you like.

Small Manure Worm

This is tied exactly the same as a San Juan worm pattern (of which there are many patterns). In this case, it is designed to imitate a small red manure worm, although your friends will probably chastise you for claiming to fish a "terrestrial" while really fishing a "San Juan worm." Who cares? The fish certainly do not and you can counter by claiming that their catches on a San Juan worm are really of trout that think they are munching on a red manure worm.

You can tie a different type of manure worm by making a coiled worm that will simulate what live worms do on a hook. To do this, first tie in a red chenille as shown but leave a long tag end.

Continue by wrapping over the tag end and the chenille to about ? the hook shank.

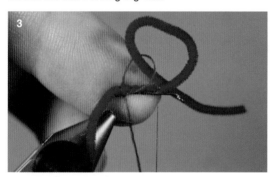

Coil the tag end of the chenille on itself as shown and then bring the tag end through the loop and around the shank as shown here.

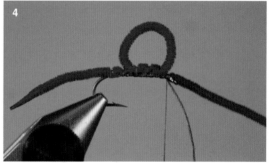

Wrap the thread to the front of the fly hook and then wrap the tag end around the loop and hook shank as shown to make the coil stay in place.

Finish by tying off the tag end of the thread, and the chenille, at the front of the fly hook. Complete with a whip finish.

Hook: Regular hook, sizes 10 to 16

Thread: Red or to match color of worm. Dark red is best to imitate a manure worm.

Body: Vernille or Ultra Chenille red or to match the color worm desired

Tying directions: Cut Vernille or Ultra Chenille to the length desired for the hook and worm being tied. With a short length of the chenille extending behind the hook, tie down the thread and the chenille at the rear of the hook. Hold the chenille parallel to the hook shank and spiral wrap over both with the thread until in back of the hook eye. Tie off on the hook shank. If necessary, trim the ends of the chenille and fuse to a tapered end by using a flame to sear the ends of the chenille.

Variations:

After tying in at the rear of the hook shank, wrap the thread forward and then follow with a wrap of the chenille that is tied off in back of the hook eye. Leave a slight tag end of chenille extending from the hook. The appearance is of a worm with a large "sex ring" in the center of the body.

Weight a worm by bending the barb on the hook, sliding on a metal bead (brass or tungsten), then tie the chenille down at the rear of the hook shank. Wrap the thread forward, spiraling over the chenille to the center-placed bead, then fold the chenille over the bead and continue to tie down until reaching the front of the hook shank.

If retrieving a worm or fishing in a current (as opposed to soaking it in a farm pond), minimize the amount of worm chenille extending from the front of the hook since this tends to fold back and look unnatural when the worm is twitched through the water.

To make a worm with a coiled section (such as real worms do in the water), tie down as above in the middle of a 2X or 3X long hook and leave a long extended tag end of thread. Wrap over the worm for about ⅔ of the shank length, then fold the worm in a circle around itself and on top of the hook shank. Use the tag end to spiral wrap over the worm several times, then tie off with the working thread. Continue to the front of the hook shank and tie off, then finish as above. The result is a worm coiled on itself in the center.

Easy imitations of worms are possible using a length of chenille or cactus chenille. To do this, tie in a length of chenille, then furl it, then tie down again as shown here. This creates a doubled tail to the worm.

Bass worm

This worm takes advantage of a furling technique to twist material to make a long tail, sort of the fly fisherman's equivalent of the hardware angler's soft plastic worm. It is a simple fly, although a little outside of the normal concept of terrestrials as thought of by trout fishermen. In small sizes it also works for crappie, perch, and other bottom feeders.

To complete the furled worm, wrap the thread forward and then wrap over the hook shank with the chenille as shown to complete the fly. Clip and tie off with a whip finish to complete.

Hook: Regular or long shank hook, sizes 6 to 2/0

Thread: Purple, red, brown, or to match the desired worm color

Body: Purple, red, brown, or other color cactus chenille or Estaz

Tying directions: Tie down the thread at the rear of the hook shank, then tie in a length of chenille about three times the length of the worm desired. Twist the chenille, *but be sure to twist it in the same direction in which it was manufactured.* (More on this and easier ways of doing it can be found in Chapter 2—Simple Tying Steps and Simple Tricks.) Hold the chenille about two-thirds from the tied end, and fold over towards the hook shank to allow this end to fold and twist on itself. Tie down the end you are holding after the twisted chenille twists on itself (furls) to make a tight tail. Then wrap the thread forward, followed by a wrap of the chenille. Tie off at the head and complete with a whip finish.

Variations:

While cactus chenille or Estaz seems to make the best material for larger worms, you can also tie it with regular chenille, or even yarn or stranded dubbing. These materials will make for thinner worms unless the material is doubled first before making the twists and tying steps above.

Tie in any color desired, with black, blue, red, and brown also popular colors.
Tie a multicolored worm by using two thin strands of two different colors of chenille or other stranded materials, and twisting and tying them down as above.

Tie weighted versions by adding a metal bead, cone head or dumb bell eye to the hook shank before tying the fly.

Tie other weighted versions by first tying down parallel strands of lead or a wrap of lead or non-lead wire for weight.

Tie rattle versions by following the above instructions, but first tying a rattle (glass, plastic, or metal) to the hook shank, then wrapping over this with the body wrap around the hook shank.

chapter

Leaf Hoppers, Katydids, Spiders, Butterflies, Caterpillars, Cicadas, Roaches, and Flies (House, Deer, Horse, Others)

Leaf hoppers, frog hoppers, plant hoppers, tree hoppers, spittle bugs, and the like are part of a large group of lesser insects that are also good terrestrial patterns. These are smaller than grasshoppers and crickets, though some resemble these larger insects; some are flat-winged and -bodied, some have highly arched bodies, some are plain, and some brightly colored. They tend to go to extremes, with some resembling a small tank, while others are long and tapered like the fuselage of an airplane

Unlike an entomologist, why worry about what kind of "hopper" it is—leaf, tree, frog, plant, or something else? The fish hardly care and the slight differences between wings, colors, length, size, and general shape cannot be dealt with using standard fly tying techniques, in any case, and would be unimportant if they could be.

Other than making these patterns small, delicate, and simple, there are no right or wrong ways to tie them and few highly specific patterns. One good rule is to tie these various hoppers in the size, color, and shape of those you find in your fishing areas. They might be bright green, short and fat, or multicolored, striped, long, and flat. Here are some possibilities to consider:

FLOATING IMITATIONS

Marinaro Jassid

When Vince Marinaro developed his simple jassid fly, he described it variously as a beetle and also a member of the jassid family—thus the name. Many writers have simply described this pattern as a leaf hopper. It seems more like a small, delicate leaf hopper pattern than a heavier, bulkier beetle pattern, but both insect families are avidly taken by trout and panfish.

Hook: Regular hook, sizes 22 to 20
Thread: Black
Legs or hackle: One to three small short-fibered hackles
Body or wing—Short, small, or medium jungle cock or similar short and sealed feather

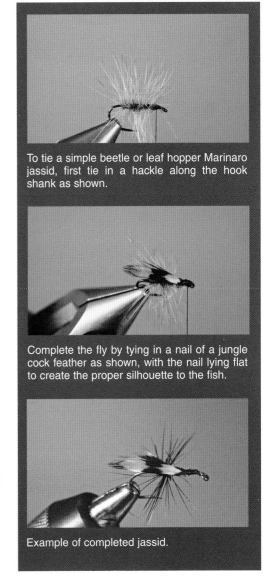

To tie a simple beetle or leaf hopper Marinaro jassid, first tie in a hackle along the hook shank as shown.

Complete the fly by tying in a nail of a jungle cock feather as shown, with the nail lying flat to create the proper silhouette to the fish.

Example of completed jassid.

Tying instructions: Tie in the thread at the head of the hook shank and then tie in a short-fibered hackle or two. Spiral back to the rear of the hook shank, then back up to the eye, and tie off. Tie down a jungle cock feather or other feather, tie off, and complete with a whip finish.

Variations:

Tie this with any small or trimmed feather other than the jungle cock of the original pattern. In doing so, pick or trim a feather that is long and slim, and coat it to seal and protect the feather using Flexament or a similar product.

Foam Leafhopper

Foam leafhoppers are tied with nothing more than a foam body and trimmed hackle for legs. They are small—generally no more than one inch long, and often mottled in color. Often a white or orange color foam base is best, mottling the finished fly with brown and black felt tip markers.

Hook: Regular hooks, sizes 20 to 14
Thread: Black or color to match pattern
Body: Sheet foam, ⅛ inch thick, in color to resemble these insects—orange, brown, tan, black, cream and yellow
Legs: Short-fibered hackle, trimmed if necessary
Tying instructions: Tie in the thread in back of the hook eye and tie down a tapered length of foam, the bulk pointed forward. Wrap the thread back to a position about ⅓ back from the hook eye, and tie in a hackle. Wrap the hackle around the hook shank and tie off, clipping excess hackle. Fold over the foam and tie down with the thread. Tie off with a whip finish and trim the hackle legs if necessary.

Folded Foam Leaf Hopper

This is similar to the above, but tied with sheet foam folded over upon itself, and then tied down on the hook shank.

Hook: Regular or 2X long hook, sizes 20 to 14
Thread: Black or to match pattern body color
Body: Thin strip of sheet foam, tapered on the ends and folded in half before being tied down. One-sided self-stick foam helps to hold the two sides together. Use colors such as white, cream, orange, yellow, light green, etc.
Legs: Brown or black hackle
Tying instructions: Tie in the thread at about ⅓ back on the hook shank and then tie down, wrap, and tie off the hackle. Closely trim the top and sides of the hackle. Fold over the foam, end to end, making sure that the tapered ends are appropriate for the hook shank length. Tie down with the thread, with the folded ends towards the rear of the fly. Tie off. If the rear part of the body flares out too much, wind the thread through the hackle and lightly tie down the rear of the body to secure it.

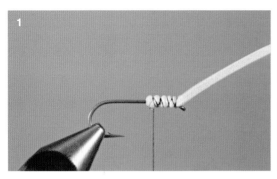

Leaf hopper, tree hoppers, frog hoppers, and similar insects are easy to tie using a variety of means. One way is to tie in a hackle and then fold over a length of foam. This simple leaf hopper is tied using a forward wrap of a thin, tapered strip of foam as shown.

In the middle of the hook shank tie in a length of clipped hackle.

Spiral wrap the hackle as shown to make the legs of the leaf hopper.

Fold the foam over the hackle and shank of the hook and tie down as shown to complete this simple leaf hopper.

Angled view of the leaf hopper showing the tapered end of the foam which simulates the tapered wings of the live insects.

Variations:

Use felt tip markers to mottle the body as a real leaf hopper would be mottled.

Quill Leafhopper—Tie as one of the above two versions, but on top of the body; or tie down a folded section of turkey feather or a section of wing quill in green, white, yellow, or similar light color. Turkey simulates the mottled appearance of these flies and is an ideal choice. Trim the forward butt ends.

SINKING IMITATIONS

Wing Quill Leafhopper

Tie as above, but use a wrapped body of yarn or stranded body material as follows:

Hook: Regular or 2X long shank, 18 to 14

Thread: Black or to match fly color

Body: Yarn or stranded body material in yellow, orange, tan, cream, brown, and light green. Some yarns that are mottled in color are ideal for this.

Legs: Brown or black hackle

Wing: Small section of turkey feather

To tie a simple leaf hopper using a different tying technique, first tie in a body of yarn as shown.

Next, tie in and wrap a hackle to form legs on the front of the fly.

Complete the leaf hopper by adding a wing of feather, turkey quill, or hackle to simulate the wings of the leaf hopper. Leaf hoppers and their kin vary widely, so don't be afraid to try similar designs and colors.

Tying instructions: Tie in the thread at about ⅓ back on the hook shank, then tie down the yarn or stranded material and wrap to the hook bend. Wrap the thread back up to the tie-in point, followed by a wrap of the yarn/stranded material. Wrap the yarn up to the eye of the hook and then back, tying off at the tie-in point. Tie in a hackle, make a few turns with it and tie off, clipping any excess. Add a short length of turkey feather, folded over to make a tent-like wing. Tie off and complete with a whip finish.

Variations:

Use a section of wing quill for the wing in place of the turkey.

Add a strip of lead or non-lead wire to sink the fly.

Chenille Leafhopper. Tie as above, using the same materials with the exception of a chenille body in place of the yarn or stranded material.

SPIDERS

Spiders are lesser species of terrestrials, but it still pays to keep one or two patterns in your box. You can tie these in any size, since spiders range from tiny examples that would be tied on size 22 hook up to large multi-colored garden spiders that can reach 1½ inches long and could be tied on 2X long size 2 hooks.

FLOATING SPIDERS

Foam Spider

Tying a foam spider is little different from tying a beetle, other than the rounded body (abdomen), small thorax and head, and long legs. Spiders are arachnids—not insects—and thus have eight legs, not six. Few patterns of any fly are exact as to leg count and the fish won't care—and can't count—anyway.

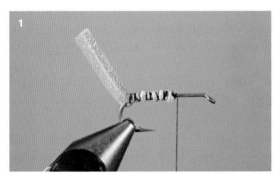

To tie a simple foam floating spider, first tie in a thin strip of foam aimed to the rear of the fly as shown.

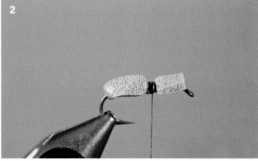

Next, wrap the thread forward and fold the foam over the hook shank and tie down for the abdomen of the spider.

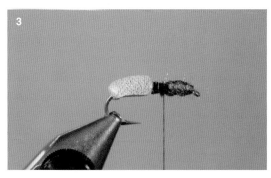

Tie in a length of yarn and then wrap forward and back to the center of the hook to make a head and thorax.

Next, tie in a hackle to make legs.

Wrap the hackle around the waist of the spider to complete the spider imitation.

Hook: Regular or 2X long hook in sizes 18 through 4

Thread: Black, brown or gray

Abdomen: Gray or brown sheet foam cut to size and shape, or preformed foam body that ties up as a fat abdomen

Thorax/head: Brown or gray yarn

Legs: Brown, black or gray hackle

Tying instructions: Tie in the thread just forward of the center of the hook with the foam pointed backwards, and wrap over the foam down to the bend of the hook. Reverse the thread wrap up to the tie-in point, then fold over the foam abdomen and tie down. Tie in a strand of yarn for the thorax, wrap up to the hook eye and back, and then tie off. Tie in a hackle and wrap it around the hook shank at the junction of the abdomen and thorax. Tie off, clip excess and complete the fly with a whip finish.

Variations:

Use any color foam, hackle and yarn you wish, since some spiders are brightly colored or mottled in appearance.

Use chenille or stranded material in place of the yarn for the thorax and head.

Yarn Spider

This pattern (Itsy Bitsy Spider) is from Fishy Fullum, and consists of a small, formed plastic bag filled with yarn and then tied in place to form a smooth-skinned spider abdomen. Because of this plastic abdomen bag, it floats. This is variation of Fishy's design; his original design is covered in the list of variations.

Hook: Regular hook, sizes 16 to 10
Thread: Black, gray or to match body and spider color
Body (abdomen): Dry cleaner plastic made into bag holding clipped yarn or dubbing fur. Best colors are black, gray, brown, dark green, etc.
Body: (thorax and head)—Chenille (small flies) or cactus chenille (larger spiders)
Legs: Rubber legs in colors to match spider—black, gray, brown
Eyes: Small black plastic bead chain from craft store
Tying instructions: Tie in thread near the rear of the hook shank. Prepare a small ball of dubbing fur or short-clipped yarn and place in dry cleaner plastic wrap to form ball. This is almost like the bait bags that hardware/bait, steelhead fishermen use. Make the ball

To tie the Fishy Fullum Itsy Bitsy spider, first push your finger or a smooth rod into a sheet of plastic to make a pocket or depression to hold dubbing material for the abdomen.

Fill the plastic pocket with dubbing or clipped yarn of your color choice and then secure the pocket and tie down as shown to make the smooth abdomen of the spider.

Wrap forward and tie in a pair of small plastic bead eyes for the spider eyes.

For the thorax tie in a length of yarn or chenille and wrap around the body and figure eight around the eyes.

Add rubber legs to the sides of the body as shown to complete the fly.

Top view of the Itsy Bitsy spider.

appropriate to the size of the spider, about 13⁄16 inch to 3⁄8 inch for the hooks listed. Tighten the plastic to make a small ball, and tie down on the hook. Clip the excess plastic. Wrap the thread forward. Tie in two small black plastic bead chain eyes near the front of the hook shank. Wrap the thread forward to the hook eye. Tie in a length of chenille or cactus chenille, then wrap the thread to just in back of the eyes. Wrap the chenille down the shank to the abdomen, then back up to the eyes and tie off. Add two strands of rubber legs on each side of the body. Complete with a whip finish.

Variations:

The original design for this is with a ball of dubbing and then waxing the thread to make a dubbing body in place of the chenille. The chenille as listed here just makes this a little easier to tie.

Tie in any size, adjusting the materials and the abdomen size accordingly. Spiders can be tiny or huge, so that anything from a size 18 up through a long shank (2X or 3X long) size 1 hook may be needed.

SINKING SPIDERS

Pom-pom Spider

This is a variation of the above design, but using a craft store pom-pom as the abdomen. It does not have the shiny appearance of the abdomen in the floating form, but does work, sinks slowly, and is a good representation of a spider shape.

Hook: Regular hook in sizes 14 through 8
Thread: Black, gray, brown—to match the body color of the spider
Body (abdomen): Black, gray or brown craft store pom-pom or white pom-pom dyed or colored with permanent felt tip marker
Body (thorax and head): Black, gray and brown cactus chenille
Legs: Rubber legs, tied into both sides
Eyes: Black craft store plastic bead chain eyes

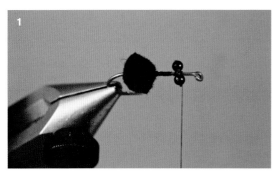

To tie an underwater spider, use a pom-pom available from craft stores. You can get these in black as shown or white and color them with a felt tip marker. Carefully slide the point of the hook through the center of the pom-pom and then position the hook in the vise. Glue the pom-pom in place with cyanoacrylate glue (fast-acting glue) and then wrap on thread and add plastic eyes as shown.

Tie in a length of peacock herl or ice chenille as shown here. Then wrap around the hook shank and figure eight around the eyes.

Complete the fly by adding rubber legs to the sides of the spider.

Tying instructions: Carefully(!) thread a pom-pom onto the hook, forcing the hook point through the center and around on the hook shank. Use cyanoacrylate glue to glue the pom-pom in place at the rear of the hook shank. Tie in thread just forward of the pom-pom and then wrap forward and tie in black eyes just in back of the hook shank. Tie in chenille at the head of the hook shank and wrap the thread down to the spider eyes. Wrap the chenille down the hook shank to the pompom and then back up to the eyes. Tie off. Tie in two strands of rubber legs on each side and tie off with a whip finish.

Variations:

In place of the pom-pom, use a larger wrap of yarn, chenille, or dubbing to make the round abdomen.

Tie in any size desired, including smaller or larger than the sizes listed above.

In larger sizes, use a white pompom and color it with bright bands or stripes including red, orange and yellow to simulate a larger garden spider.

BUTTERFLIES

Butterflies are a little-used terrestrial, basically for two reasons. First, while they can be flying over and falling into water, they are taken far less often and are thus less important than the ants, beetles, hoppers and crickets that make up much of the terrestrial fly box. Second, if tied with typical butterfly wings, they are a horror to cast. The mass to air resistance ratio makes them too light and air resistant so that they drag through the air and do not turn over easily—or sometimes at all. There is one exception to all this—the Hewitt skater—a butterfly imitation.

This fly has no body, but a lot of wing with the two mating hackles that make it a large-hackled fly, but even this was difficult to cast. Hewitt noted that it was best if cast with at least 40 feet of line in the air. This much line also allowed him to drop the fly "like a feather" and then jump and dance the fly over the water surface without it sinking. He sometimes found that trout would jump over or miss the fly when it was danced this way, and soon discovered that the best technique was to slowly retrieve line to draw the fly carefully over the surface, so that the fish could hit it solidly.

Hewitt Skater (Butterfly Pattern)

Hook: Dry fly hook of any brand, sizes 14 and 16 (other sizes possible, but these are the best and original pattern—Hewitt tied it first on a size 16 light Model Perfect hook)

Thread: Black

Hackle: Two large brown hackles

Tying instructions: Use two large hackles that are tied face to face in the center of a light wire hook. Tie by securing the thread to the center of the hook shank, then tie in a large hackle with about a one-inch fiber to make a fly of about a two-inch diameter. Tie the fly with the dull or concave side forward, followed by a second hackle tie with the dull or concave side facing the rear. The original called for a sparse tie, but you can make these ties as sparse or as full as you like. Push the tied hackle together to make them into one mating hackle mass, then tie off and complete. The only special considerations of this fly are that you choose a dry fly hackle (little webbing). Also, note that the hackle is wrapped in at one spot. Use your finger/thumb nails to push the two hackles together to make a tight hackle wrap.

To tie a Hewitt butterfly, tie an oversize hackle to the midpoint on the hook shank. First tie and wrap one hackle and then a second, with both of them mating at the center of the hook.

Here the hackle has been wrapped around the hook shank to tie the Hewitt-style butterfly.

Variations:

Add a long tail to the hook shank, prior to wrapping in the two hackles, to make another fly that is really an oversized variant. The addition of this long tail makes this a completely different fly, but one that still alights slowly and gently on the surface to take big trout. Hewitt did note that the addition of a tail does change the movement of the fly on the water.

Tie the fly in something other than the original brown color. Butterflies come in many wing colors. Yellow, orange, white, tan, light olive, and grizzly are other colors that would match many butterflies.

CATERPILLARS

Caterpillars are the larval form of butterflies and moths found along streamside brush, shrubs, flowers, and trees where they fall in and make a juicy meal for any fish. They are popular for trout fishing, but should not be ignored for bass. They are generally too big for sunfish unless tied in very small sizes, but can be used for crappie, perch and other species when they are taking off the surface. Most caterpillars are fat with hairy projections, or setae. In some cases these setae cover the entire larval insect, while in others they are only at the ends or sparsely located on the body.

FLOATING CATERPILLARS

Foam Caterpillar

Foam can be used for caterpillars by threading it on the hook, wrapping it around the hook shank, or folding it on the hook shank and tying it down with segmented wraps. Threading the foam onto the hook shank is more gluing that fly tying, although you can add a hackle wrap on each end to dress it up a bit. You can also tie it with a segmented body, but this may be hard with some of the dense foams sold for some fly tying applications. One favorite method is to cut ⅛ inch thick sheet foam into a strip about ⅛ inch wide, then tie down one end and wrap it around the hook shank just as you would a body of chenille. With a palmered hackle wrap over this, the result is a very caterpillar-like fly. Sometimes I leave the hackle long; other times I clip it to make it spiky and more like some caterpillars found along the waters edge.

Hook: 4X long shank hook, sizes 6 to 1, depending upon size of caterpillar desired
Thread: Black or to match color of caterpillar
Body: Sheet foam, appropriate to size of caterpillar and hook, in any color desired. Popular colors are yellow, brown, orange, green, and black
Legs: Palmered saddle hackle, usually contrasting color to that of the caterpillar body. Black and brown are popular.
Tying instructions: Tie in the thread at the front of the hook shank and tie down a hackle or two for palmering up the hook shank. Wrap the thread to the rear of the hook shank. Prepare a length of sheet foam that you can fold over lengthwise and still tie on top of the hook shank so that the hackle (legs) protrude down and suggest a caterpillar. Palmer the

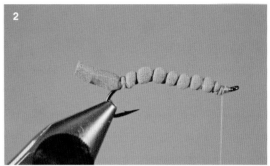

One way to tie a simple caterpillar is to carefully thread the hook point lengthwise through the body of foam. It helps to have the hook secured in a vise, as shown, to prevent accidents.

Once the foam is threaded onto the hook shank, it is easy to tie on thread and then spiral wrap up the hook shank to segment the body of the caterpillar. It is also possible to add a hackle for palmering up the hook shank to make setae on the caterpillar.

hackle down and around the hook shank and tie off at the rear of the hook shank with the thread. Hold and fold the foam, wrap over it with the thread and then around the hook shank for two or three turns. Make two more wraps around the foam, holding it so that it is above and on top of the hook shank to allow the hackle to show. Continue this way up the hook shank until the foam is wrapped around and on the entire hook. Tie off at the head of the hook and complete the fly with a whip finish.

Variations:

If desired, clip the hackle to make the legs short like those found on a real caterpillar.

Use a foam cylinder in place of the sheet foam. Often this is easier if you flatten one side of the foam cylinder and use some epoxy or cyanoacrylate glue on this side to glue and seat on the top of the hook shank.

Tie in any color desired, with popular colors yellow, light green, brown, tan, cream, orange, and even red.

For the banded appearance of some caterpillars, use a fine felt tip marker to make horizontal or vertical color bands on the foam body.

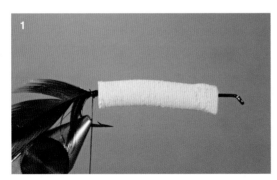

Threading a cylinder onto a hook shank makes it possible to make a simple hackle-wrapped caterpillar. Here the foam cylinder has been threaded onto the hook and a hackle tied in at the rear.

The caterpillar is completed by spiral wrapping the hackle around the foam body as shown and tying off at the head.

Hook: 4X long hook, sizes 8 to 2

Thread: Black or to match caterpillar color desired

Foam: Sheet foam or foam cylinder as with above caterpillar imitation. Soft foams are best to allow for palmering and for segmenting the foam body.

Hackle: Black or brown saddle hackle, although any color can be used.

Tying instructions: Tie in thread at the rear of the fly, then tie in one or two long saddle hackles. Position the foam body over the hook shank. If using sheet foam folded over, it can be wrapped around the hook shank to allow the hackle to palmer the entire body to simulate setae. If using a foam cylinder, slice it lengthwise so that it envelops the hook shank. With a foam cylinder, wrap the hook shank with thread and then coat with cyanoacrylate glue or a thin coat of epoxy after tying in the saddle hackle and before adding the foam around the hook shank. Spiral wrap with thread over the body as you progress up the hook, or make two turns around the body (foam sheet), then several turns around only the hook shank, then two more turns around the body. Continue this way up the hook shank. Once the body is in place, palmer the hackle up and around the body until the front of the hook is reached. Tie off with the thread and complete the fly with a whip finish.

An easy way to tie a simple caterpillar is to tie in a hackle (to palmer in setae for the insect) and then fold a strip of foam over the hook shank. Here, in preparation of this tie, a hackle has been tied in place on the rear of the hook shank.

Begin to add the body by cutting a strip of foam to size as with the brown caterpillar being tied here. Then fold the foam over the hook shank and tie down with spiral or sequential wraps (see text for details) around the body as you work forward.

Continue tying this way towards the head of the fly, as shown here.

To make it easy to tie and to get equal segments while tying, use your thumb as shown to "mark" the position of the next wrap around each segment of the body.

Once the end of the hook is reached, clip and tie off the foam as shown here.

Complete the caterpillar by spiral wrapping (palmering) the hackle around the foam body as shown and then tying off at the head of the fly.

Variations:

Clip or trim the hackle as desired. For this, you can trim the entire hackle or just trip the top and leave the bottom long, or vice-versa.

Wrap hackle down at both ends of the hook shank and then wrap the hackle around only those ends to simulate some caterpillars that have setae only or primarily at the ends. Tie on a curved hook to simulate a caterpillar curling up in the water. An example would be the Mustad 37160 hook, but many others are available.

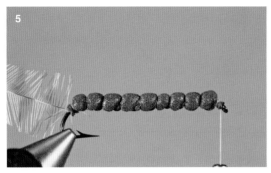

One way to capitalize on the way caterpillars writhe around is to use a curved hook as shown. Here, a hackle, and then a thin strip of foam, have been tied down, with the foam spiral-wrapped around the hook.

Continue the fly by wrapping the hackle (palmering it) up the hook and around the foam body.

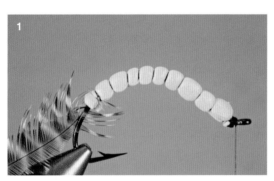

Wrap the hackle to the eye of the hook and then tie off as shown.

Completed caterpillar on curved shank hook. In this case, a Mustad 37160 hook has been used.

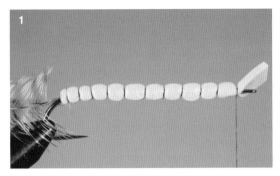

Steps in making a foam caterpillar, here on a straight shank hook; first the hackle is tied in place and the foam wrapped around the hook shank and secured with spiral wraps of thread.

Underside of the hook with the foam in place, showing how the foam wraps completely around the hook shank during the tying process.

Wrapping the hackle forward to the eye of the hook and tying off.

Completed caterpillar on straight shank hook.

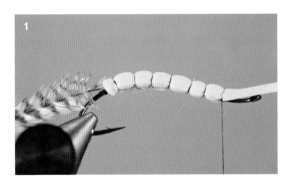

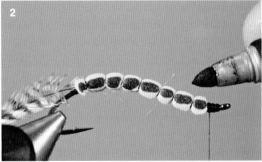

Many caterpillars have bands of dots of contrasting color on their bodies. Here is how to tie an imitation of one of these. First tie in a hackle and then wrap a foam body around the hook shank as shown.

To make the color bands, mark the foam with a felt tip marker. Here, black bands are made along the side of the caterpillar body. This can be done on the sides, top, bottom or on only parts of the body.

Completed caterpillar with the hackle wrapped in place and color bands showing. A similar look is made possible with Bill Skilton USA-Flies striped foam.

To tie a caterpillar with the legs under it and with no setae, first spiral wrap a clipped hackle along the hook shank. Reverse the thread by carefully weaving it back through the hackle to the rear of the hook shank.

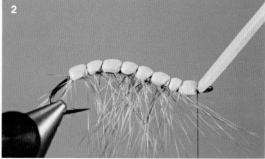

Then slightly fold the hackle down over the hook shank and place a thin strip of foam on top and spiral wrap with thread to segment the body.

Clip off any excess foam and then complete with a whip finish. The completed caterpillar has clipped hackle for legs and no setae on the body.

SINKING CATERPILLAR PATTERNS

Chenille Caterpillar

Hook: 4X long shank hook, sizes 6 to 1/0

Thread: Black or to match caterpillar body

Body: Thin or thick chenille, depending upon shape and size of caterpillar, with color to match the caterpillar desired. Popular colors are yellow, orange, cream, tan, light green, and white.

Hackle: Black or brown saddle hackle, long or trimmed

Tying instructions: Tie in the thread and at the rear of the hook shank tie in one or two long saddle hackles. Tie in the length of chenille. Wrap the thread forward to just in back of the hook eye. Wrap the chenille up to the hook eye and tie off. Palmer the hackle around the chenille body to the hook eye and tie off.

Variations:

Trim the hackle short if desired.

Trim hackle short on top and leave long (untrimmed) on bottom for different look to legs and setae.

Tie with heavy yarn or stranded body material such as Gudebrod EZ-Body in place of the chenille

For a smooth look, use Ultra Chenille or Vernille in place of the chenille.

To tie flies with clipped hackle, it is easier to clip the hackle first before tying it onto the hook. It also makes for more even results this way.

Examples of three sizes and colors of foam caterpillars.

Underwater caterpillars are easy to tie using the same techniques above, except with yarn or dubbing bodies in place of foam. Here a caterpillar is being tied using a hackle and with a tied-in and wrapped yarn body.

The underwater caterpillar is completed by wrapping the hackle forward as shown and tying off at the head of the fly.

Another example of an underwater caterpillar. Here the hackle and yarn have been tied in place.

Here the yarn has been wrapped forward to be followed by the hackle.

The nearly completed caterpillar is tied off at the head with the hackle serving as setae on the body.

Completed short caterpillar.

Furled Chenille Caterpillar

This results in a slightly longer caterpillar with the furled chenille body.

Hook: 2X to 4X long, sizes 6 to 1/0
Thread: Black or to match caterpillar color
Body: Thin or thick chenille, in yellow, tan, cream, light green, orange, and white.
Hackle: Black or brown saddle hackle, long or trimmed
Tying instructions: Tie as before, by tying in the thread and then tying down saddle hackles and chenille. Begin by twisting the chenille (in the twist direction in which it was made), then fold it over on itself to make for a short furled end. Tie down the folded end on the hook shank and then wrap the chenille to the hook eye. Palmer the hackle around the body to the hook eye and tie off. Complete with a whip finish.

Variations:
Consider the same variations as basic chenille caterpillar.

You can also tie caterpillars with extended furled bodies. Here a length of chenille has been furled and tied down to the rear of the hook shank, then the hackle tied in place.

Completed extended body caterpillar.

Fore and Aft Chenille Caterpillar

This is a major variation, also with some changes in tying style, thus it is treated here as a separate pattern.

Hook: 4X long in sizes 6 through 1
Thread: Black or to match caterpillar color
Body: Chenille in yellow, white, cream, tan, light green, orange or red
Hackle: Black or brown hackle
Tying instructions: Tie in the thread at the rear of the hook leaving a long tag end uncut. Tie in one or two hackle feathers. Tie in the chenille. Wrap the thread forward to the end of the hook. Tie in a hackle feather. Wrap the chenille forward to the eye of the hook. Tie off and cut the excess. Wrap the rear hackle a few turns up around the body and then back to the rear. Tie off with the tag end of thread, trim the hackle and complete this tie with a whip finish. Wrap the forward hackle back down the body for two turns and then back up to the hook eye. Tie off, trim the hackle and complete the fly with a whip finish. This makes a caterpillar that has legs and setae on both ends, but lacking in the middle. Many caterpillars are like this—in addition to those that have legs and setae the full length of the body.

CICADAS

Cicadas are often thought to occur only every 17 years. Actually, some occur every year, on staggered schedules of that cycle, and with some on other cycles, such as a 13-year cycle. As a result of these irregular (but often annual) occurrences, imitations of cicadas are good to try every summer. Most fish are only interested in something that looks good to eat. The lack of a cicada history does not affect the efficiency of such imitations. Fish strike and eat insects—including cicadas—instinctively, based on other respective evolutionary and genetic history traits.

These are some simple imitations that are good, starting with a design of mine that is particularly imitative of a cicada, simple to tie and effective to fish.

Floating Cicada

This is tied not to imitate the bulk of a cicada, but to imitate the silhouette of the insect as fish see a cicada. It is still easy to cast without the cigar butt-bulk of the real insect or a more exact imitation.

To tie a cicada, first cut and shape two sections of foam—one white or cream and one brown or dark green. These should be slightly rounded at one end.

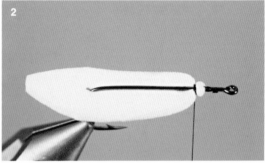

Slip the hook through the rear of the white foam body as shown and then place the hook in the vise.

Tie on the thread, and tie down the front of the white foam; then tie in a hackle and also the other brown/green foam pointed towards the front of the fly.

Fold the brown/green foam over as shown and tie down to form a head and also to position the hackle under the foam as legs.

Tie in clear wings of clear, sheet wing material as shown.

Add eyes using a nozzle-style fabric paint dispenser to complete the fly.

Example of a real cicada and a floating foam imitation designed by the author. Note that this is a different imitation than the one tied in this series of illustrations, and uses cactus chenille for the legs.

Example of a floating cicada tied with cactus chenille legs in place of hackle.

Hook: Size 2 to 1/0, 2X long

Thread: Black or brown

Belly: White, cream or tan ⅛ inch sheet foam, cut to long oval shape

Back: Brown, dark green or black ⅛ inch sheet foam, cut to long oval shape.

Hackle: Black or brown hackle to simulate legs

Wings: Flash material such as Krystal flash or Flashabou, or thin clear or whitish packing foam, cut to wing shape

Eyes: Orange or red dot of fabric paint

Tying instructions: Cut the foam to size and cicada shape, just slightly longer than the length of the hook shank, with the dark back foam slightly longer than the light-colored belly foam. Position the light-color abdomen foam over the hook shank with the forward edge about ⅓ shank length in back of the hook eye. Note the position of the beginning of the hook bend and mark this on the foam. Use an awl or bodkin to punch a hole in the foam at this mark, and run the hook point through it. Place the hook in the vise and tie in thread at the head of the hook shank. Slide the foam around and tie the forward part down about ⅓ shank length shank length in back of the hook eye. Tie in a hackle and wrap it around the hook shank to form legs. Tie in the dark foam, facing forward and wrap over it to the hook eye, then reverse the thread back to the tie-down point. Fold the dark foam back over the light foam and tie down gently. Tie in the wing material of cut and shaped sheet packing foam or stranded flash material. Clip off any excess forward, tie a whip finish and complete the fly. Use flexible glue (rubber cement, Pliobond or Ultra Flex) to glue the two layers of sheet foam. For the wings, add glue to the underside to hold them in place on the foam back. Finish by adding a dot of color to each side of the head to simulate eyes.

Variations:

Use light colors of light green or tan felt tip to mark the belly of the fly with the markings/striations of a live cicada.

It is usually not necessary, but if desired, add a dot of bright colored foam (tied or glued) to the top of the cicada for visibility and as a strike indicator.

BF (Barely Floating) Cicada

Floating cicadas are more fun to fish, but sinking cicadas are effective and buggy to attract any fish after a large meal or mouthful. These are similar but simpler to tie than the floating version. The main difference is that these may float for a while, but may also slowly sink and drift in the current. They can be twitched through still water.

An example of a BF or Barely Floating Cicada. This uses cactus chenille for the body and just a thin foam wing material made from packing-sheet foam. The result is that it floats low in the water, and is often more realistic in presentation.

Hook: Size 2 to 1/0, 2X long
Thread: Black or brown
Body: Tan, cream or light green cactus chenille or Estaz.
Head: Same as body
Hackle: Black or brown
Wings: Thin sheet packing foam or clear sheet plastic wing material.
Tying instructions: Tie in thread at the rear of the hook shank, then tie down the body material of Estaz or cactus chenille. Wrap the thread forward to a point about 1/3 shank length in back of the hook eye. Wrap the chenille forward, past the thread, and to the hook eye, then back to the tie down point. Tie off and clip excess. Tie in a hackle and wrap around the hook shank, then tie off and clip the excess. Tie in the wings of stranded flash material or shaped and sized foam packing, clip the forward excess and tie off. Tie a whip finish to complete and clip thread. Add some flexible glue to the body to secure the wings to the chenille body. Note that the thin sheet foam plastic packing material floats the fly, but floats low in the surface film. This, basically, is how a cicada floats or rides in the water on the surface until it ultimately sinks; thus, the name—BF for barely floating—and the result, a very natural cicada imitation. It makes a big mouthful for any trout, or smallmouth or largemouth bass.

Variations:

Add a bead or cone head for weight if desired to sink the fly and get deep. This can be plastic, glass, metal (brass, steel) or tungsten, depending on the weight and depth desired. Add lead or non-lead dumb bell eyes and wrap the chenille around them figure eight style to form a head, then add red, yellow or orange eyes to the lead eyes to simulate the eyes of a live cicada.

Use regular chenille in place of the cactus chenille if you wish a less fuzzy look. Palmer hackle along and over the body chenille for a different look (tie on first), then clip on top before gluing any sheet foam wings in place.

ROACHES, FLIES—HOUSE, DEER, HORSE FLIES AND OTHERS

FLOATING PATTERNS
Floating Firefly

There are far fewer fireflies in many areas now than in the past, but they still make a good terrestrial. They are particularly good for evening fishing when they start to fly and can end up in the drink. This is a simple pattern taking advantage of the many phosphorescent materials on the market today for the cold-light tail of these insects.

Hook: 2X long shank hook, sizes 14 to 10
Thread: Black
Body rear: Chartreuse or yellow phosphorescent stranded material (yarn, stranded dubbing, chenille, etc.) or same color fluorescent materials as a second choice.

To tie a lightning bug, first tie in a length of thin black foam, then a length of body cactus chenille and plain chenille for the rear cold light and the rest of the body.

Wrap the plain chenille up the hook shank and over the cactus chenille as show and tie off at the midpoint of the shank. Clip the plain chenille. For this, you can use phosphorescent or yellow chenille.

Continue to wrap the thread forward and then wrap and tie off the cactus chenille as shown.

Clip the excess cactus chenille.

Fold the foam over the body and tie down to complete the lightning bug imitation.

Body forward: Black ice or cactus chenille

Hackle: Black, trimmed short

Wing case—Black thin (0.5 or 1.0 mm) sheet foam, cut to shape and size

Tying instructions: Tie in thread in mid-shank, then tie in wing case foam and wrap to rear of the hook shank. Tie in the black ice chenille and then the phosphorescent material for the cold light of the firefly. Wrap the thread forward over the black ice chenille to ⅓ of the hook length and then wind forward the phosphorescent material and tie off. Clip the excess phosphorescent material and wrap the thread forward to a short distance in back of the hook eye. Wrap the ice chenille forward, tie off and clip excess. Tie in a black hackle, wrap around the hook shank and tie off. Pull the thin foam wing case forward and tie off, then clip the excess. Tie off with a whip finish and trim the hackle short to resemble the short legs of the firefly.

Variations:

If phosphorescent material is not available for the rear "cold light" of the firefly, use yellow or chartreuse fluorescent material.

A fishing tip is to use a small flashlight or inexpensive photo flash to light up the phosphorescent tail to make this terrestrial more lifelike and visible.

BF Firefly

The BF stands for barely floating, so that this is another fly that floats within the surface film—not on top of it—and perhaps ultimately sinks.

Hook: 2X long, sizes 12 to 8

Thread: Black

Rear body: Phosphorescent stranded material in yellow or chartreuse. Second choice is fluorescent body material in the same colors

Forward body: Black ice chenille

Hackle: Black, trimmed

Wing case: Black raffia or Swiss straw

Tying instructions: Tie as above for the floating firefly, except use Swiss straw for the wing case that is pulled over the body and tied down at the front to simulate the wings.

Variations:
Use two or three strands of black deer hair on each side of the body for legs as a substitute for the trimmed black hackle.

Foam Roach

The foam roach is a minor terrestrial and tied similar to and thus resembling some of the longer beetles tried. It is very similar in fly tying design to a black click beetle, except tied in dark or mahogany brown. These are flattened insects that can be small or large and tied big or small, depending you're your preference and the roach population in your fishing neighborhood.

Hook: 2X to 3X long hook, sizes 12 to 6
Thread: Brown
Body: Brown or mahogany stranded material such as E-Z Dub or braid materials such as those made by Gudebrod and Kreinik
Hackle: Brown, trimmed short
Wing case: Thin foam (0.5 or 1.0 mm) cut to shape and size.
Tying instructions: Tie in the thread in mid-shank, then tie down the thin foam pointed rearward, and wrap to the rear of the hook shank. Tie in the stranded body material and wrap the thread forward to a short distance in back of the hook eye. Wrap the body material forward and tie off, clipping the excess material. Tie in a brown hackle, make several wraps and tie off, clipping the excess. Pull the foam wing case over the tie down and tie off with a whip finish.

Variations:
For a variation with legs, palmer the hackle up and down the body before tying off and pulling the wing case into position.
Trim the hackle short to more closely resemble roach legs.

House Fly. These are typical flies that we encounter anywhere—even outside of our homes. They are usually small although sometimes in the fall we encounter larger flies. Tie house fly patterns in any size using a basic pattern with some small changes making the difference between small and larger deer flies, horse flies and blue bottle flies. Tie these with slight changes of foam and chenille/yarn bodies for sinking and floating patterns.

To tie a floating house fly, the steps are very similar to that of tying a winged ant. First tie in a strip of black foam followed by several lengths of peacock herl.

Then wrap the thread forward followed by the peacock herl. Tie off the peacock herl.

Fold the foam over and tie down at the head and then reverse the thread to tie in the clear wings as shown.

It is also possible to tie wet fly underwater versions of this house fly using peacock herl or ice chenille and no foam as shown in this example.

Floating House Fly

This is tied in small sizes with minimal materials, but still makes for a very effective fly.

Hook: Regular hook, size 16 to 12

Thread: Black

Body: Peacock herl

Back: Thin foam (one mm thick)

Head: Folded thin foam

Wings: Stranded flash material or transparent wing material

Hackle (legs): Black, a few wraps

Tying instructions: Tie in the working thread at the rear of the hook shank, then tie down a cut and prepared long strip of thin foam. Make this about twice the length of the hook shank. Tie in a length of peacock herl and wrap the thread forward. Wrap the peacock herl forward and tie off, then fold over the foam and tie down. Continue to wrap the thread forward over the foam and then reverse the thread back to the rear of the head area. Fold the foam over and back to form the head and tie off. Tie in the wings of transparent wing material or stranded flash material. Tie in a hackle and wrap a few turns around the hook shank, then tie off and clip the excess. Complete with a whip finish and clip the excess thread.

Variations:

Tie as above, but tie in the hackle at the rear of the hook shank and then palmer it up the hook over the body and tie off before forming the head and tying down the wings and hackle.

Tie in the wings before folding the head form back over and tying down. This covers the tie-down point of the wings, and make for a neater fly, although the difference is not noticeable to fish.

Use black micro ice chenille in place of the peacock herl.

Use black Gudebrod E-Z Dub for the body.

Horse Fly. Horse flies are larger versions of the typical house fly, and far more bothersome (and painful when they bite). The tying for them is very similar to tying the house fly, except on larger hooks.

Floating Horse Fly

This is tied in larger sizes than a house fly.

Hook: Regular hook, sizes 10 to 6
Thread: Black
Body: Black cactus chenille or Estaz
Back: Thin sheet foam (⅛ inch)
Wings: Stranded flash material or thin film wing material
Hackle: Black
Tying instructions: Tie in the thread, then the tapered length of foam strip at the rear of the hook shank. Tie in the body of black chenille and wrap the thread forward to a point at ⅔ of the hook shank. Wrap the chenille forward and tie off, then fold the foam over the body and tie down. Wrap over the foam to the eye of the hook, then back to the tie-down point. Wrap the chenille forward and back and then fold the foam back over the chenille head and tie down. Tie on the wings or wing material, trim the excess and then tie in and wrap a hackle. Complete the fly with a whip finish.

Variations:

Some horse flies are dark green or blue (green-bottle or blue-bottle flies). Tie some with a dark iridescent green or bright blue ice chenille or cactus chenille.

Palmer the hackle up and over the body after tying it on at the rear in place of tying it at the head of the fly.

SINKING PATTERNS

Sinking House Fly

This is a variation of the above, tied without foam but otherwise similar.

Hook: Regular hook, sizes 12 and 14
Thread: Black
Body: Peacock herl
Head: Doubled layer of peacock herl

Hackle: Black

Wings: Stranded flash or transparent wing material

Tying instructions: Tie in the working thread at the rear, then tie down the peacock herl. Wrap the thread forward to a point about ⅔ the length of the hook shank. Wrap the peacock herl to this point and then forward to the hook eye and back down to the tie off point. Tie off and clip any excess peacock herl. Tie in the wing material of stranded flash or transparent wing material. Tie in a hackle and wrap a few turns, then tie off and clip the excess. Complete with a whip finish.

Variations:

Tie with black micro ice chenille

Tie with black E-Z Dub for the body and head

Add a black bead to the hook before tying to add weight for this sinking version of a house fly.

Tie in the hackle at the rear and then palmer it forward to form the legs.

Sinking Horse Fly

Hook: Regular hook, sizes 10 to 6

Thread: Black

Body: Black cactus chenille

Head: Double layer of black cactus chenille

Wings: Stranded flash material or wing material

Hackle: Black

Tying instructions: Tie in the thread and then the black cactus chenille at the rear of the hook shank. Wrap the thread forward to the ⅔ point of the hook shank, followed by the chenille. Continue to wrap the chenille forward and then back to the thread, then tie off the chenille. Tie in the wings, add a wrapped hackle and tie off the fly with a whip finish.

Variations:

Palmer the hackle up from the rear of the fly in place of tying it at the head.

Tie with dark green cactus chenille to simulate those flies that are dark green in color.

chapter

FISHING METHODS AND TECHNIQUES

Think of terrestrials and you often think of trout fishing and fishing in fast flowing streams and creeks, but it can also be good on cold, still-water lakes and ponds. The running water/trout fishing scenario is where much of the history and development of terrestrials originated, but there is equally good fishing with terrestrials, in both running and still waters, for smallmouth and sometimes largemouth bass, bluegills and sunfish, crappie and other panfish, even fallfish and carp.

Pond fishing for bluegills or other sunfish is a great way to spend a summer evening. Largemouth lake fishing, done by casting cicada and hopper imitations in a pad-laced cove, results in bigger catches and even bigger terrestrial fishing thrills.

The emphasis on trout in running water does not mean that you will not find other species in creeks, streams and rivers. It just seems that terrestrial fishing in running water for smallmouth, panfish, sunfish, largemouth, crappie, and a bunch of other species sadly has been ignored over the years. In most cases, fishing for species other than trout is similar to trout fishing, except for some subtle changes and adjustments in tackle, techniques and flies.

Tackle and accessories for terrestrial fishing. One problem with suggestions about tackle is that terrestrials can range from a tiny size 18 ant (or even smaller) to a large size 2 hopper or cicada. In most cases, you want the rod, line and leader matched to the fly. In running water situations, most of the terrestrials used to mach the naturals are small, even with the hoppers that typically range from about size 10 through 14.

Larger imitations, however, are also possible—and probable—for some species, some waters and some seasons. The large imitations and necessary heavier tackle typically occur late in the summer or early fall. Cicadas come out in mid summer and by late fall hoppers have had a chance to grow. Western rivers also typically have insects larger than those in the east. There, bigger is better.

Basics for picking the right outfit are: think first of the largest fly that might be used in a given situation; match that to the proposed leader necessary to fish that fly; then match that to the line necessary to carry and turn over the fly/leader combination; and finally match the rod necessary to carry and cast that line. Thus, for typical terrestrial fishing for small flies (size 12 or smaller) typical of running water, pick a leader with a 4X, 5X or smaller tippet.

You can—and should—go smaller with the tippet as you go to imitations smaller than size 10 flies, down to an 7X or 8X tippet for the tiniest flies such as ants or beetles in sizes 18 and smaller. Realize also that in many cases, fish are more aggressive when attacking terrestrials than when sipping in a mayfly. This means that if anything, you might want to err on the side of slightly heavier tackle for the heavier tippet that you might want to use, or might need to use, with aggressive fish to prevent break-offs.

Once you pick the leader and tippet size, pick the line that can easily turn over that leader and fly. Then and only then pick the rod to match the line, choosing the rod length based on your fishing and personal preference.

Some suggested examples for tippet, leader and line size are as follows:

TIPPET SIZE	TIPPET TEST	FLY HOOK SIZE
8X	1.0–1.8 lbs	20–28
7X	1.1–2.5	18–26
6X	1.4–3.5	14–22
5X	2.4–4.8	10–18
4X	3.1–6.0	8–16
3X	3.8–8.5	6–14
2X	4.5–11.5	4–8

Note that the size of the fly might vary from the above, since terrestrial flies vary more widely in their mass/air resistance characteristics than do most trout flies. For example, some ant and hopper patterns probably cast no differently than any trout fly of the same hook size. Some beetle and cicada patterns might cast differently, with a jerkier cast, as a result of their bulky body that creates a little air resistance.

Anglers vary widely as to their choice of rod length. Those fishing tiny terrestrials on small limestone streams, such as used to be popular on Pennsylvania's LeTort, often like short rods in the 5'6" to 7' range. Those dapping or fishing larger flies or who need longer casts are better off with long rods, with 9' to 9'6" being the most popular. My choice for most terrestrial fishing—and indeed most fly fishing—is for a nine-foot rod that allows me the maximum easy casting distance and plenty of shock absorbency in the rod to prevent break-offs with fine leader tippets. Long rods also have the length to easily hold up a back cast over brush or to punch out a long cast when wading deep or tubing. The long rod has an added advantage of being able to hold a fish away from the bank when fishing a pond or big river so that you can control and lead the fish as you wish during the landing process.

Species caught on terrestrials. Terrestrial fishing is best for those freshwater species that hit on the surface or occasionally take bait off the top. This does not mean that you will never catch largemouth in brackish water on crickets, stripers in saltwater bays on large beetle patterns, or white perch on sinking bee patterns, but it is the exception to the rule. Terrestrials just do not fall or fly that far out into salt or brackish water.

Bottom feeding fish, such as most of the catfish, carp, freshwater drum, and such, are seldom likely to take a terrestrial unless it is fished deep; while that's possible, it takes much of the surface fishing fun out of terrestrial fishing. You might as well be fishing a nymph or streamer.

Trout—as evidenced by the many articles and books on the subject—are on the top of the list for terrestrial fishing. Perhaps next in order would be bass, both smallmouth and largemouth, probably running neck and neck with panfish and bluegills. Other species, including perch and crappie, follow. These may or may not be popular terrestrial species depending on fishing conditions and interest in a particular geographic area.

It is important to realize that you have to fish terrestrials where fish are capable of taking them on the surface, or as a struggling or slow-sinking imitation. It is also best—though not necessary—to fish terrestrials where they are an important or possible food source. It is important to be sensible about the fishing and the species sought. Casting a beetle when fishing a pike lake might occasionally get you a strike, but is not nearly as effective as fishing a big perch streamer imitation. Pike eat perch—they do not normally go after the tiny hors d'oeuvres of beetles, ants, hoppers and crickets.

Trout are high on the list because they deserve it. They take everything and anything on the surface, including all the terrestrials listed in this book and their imitations. They typically look up from their watery world to take aquatic insects such as mayflies, caddis, and stoneflies. Taking anything that resembles a meal, including stuff originating from the stream banks, brush, and trees, is natural for them. It is similar for bass, since both smallmouth and largemouth look up to take everything, from mayflies, dragonflies, and damselflies, to downed and drowning baby birds out of the nest, mice, snakes, frogs, surface-flopping minnows, and other top water meals. Bass bugs similar in design and action to frogs, mice, snakes, and other baits have long been in vogue and a staple of bass fly fishing. In with this are terrestrials—primarily grasshoppers, crickets, cicadas, and the larger beetles that are prime meals and snacks for bass and that can be imitated easily with terrestrial patterns. Naturally, terrestrial imitations of these are accepted readily by largemouth and smallmouth bass.

Use terrestrials anywhere you like, but keep in mind that they are and have been most effective in waters into which the naturals you are imitating fall, and when fishing for fish that typically take off the surface, or at least high in the water column.

Choosing the right terrestrial. While sometimes there can be huge swarms of terrestrial insects, there is not the regular "hatch" we associate with mayflies, caddis, and stone flies. Swarms typically include flying ants, sometimes flying beetles, grasshoppers (remember the horde of locusts described in the Bible), butterflies, cicadas, bees, and wasps, etc. These are not regular, however, as are the aquatic insect hatches that can be plotted and graphed, the times and appearances of which can be found in many books on the subject, often broken down to eastern or western hatches, sometimes even states or parts of states or even river systems.

Thus, choosing the right terrestrial imitation to throw on the water first can involve anything from a good guess to the success of the most recent trip on the same water, from suggestions of a buddy (or fly shop) with the most recent experience on the water or area to what insects you see a lot of when first arriving and reading the water. It can even involve blind casting when there is no evidence of terrestrials in the area or on the water. Remember that fish are opportunistic feeders, and will take or try anything that resembles a meal.

Lacking any substantive information on what to use, assuming that you are going to fish terrestrials, start by reading the water, watching takes for those fish gulping off of the surface or cruising and searching for a meal. In this regard, you can also use binoculars to examine certain river drifts and currents for insects, or try to catch or spot what is in the air around you, knowing that some of them are going to zig when they should zag, or just lose momentum and end up in the drink. From then on, they are fish food.

Another alternative is to lie down on the bank and closely examine the water for the insects in the detritus that is drifting downstream. This is what Charlie Fox and Vince Marinaro did on the LeTort over 50 years ago to develop the basic terrestrials. What is close to the bank is likely also to be out in the center of the stream or river, thus giving you a good clue as to what to start with and in what size. You won't get as good an idea on the terrestrial population on still waters of ponds and lakes, but close examination of the water can still lead you to the best insects to imitate.

MATCHING THE NON-HATCH

Lacking everything else and lacking seeing or suspecting anything of terrestrial form on the water or taken by the fish, start with a large size basic terrestrial, such as an ant, grasshopper, cricket, beetle or bee. By fishing a large size of the chosen terrestrial imitation, you can see it better, watch for a fish's reaction to it as it floats downstream, use a larger tippet to help to prevent break-offs, and usually cast more accurately than with a tiny ant or beetle. The tiny fly might better turn over the leader, but the wind can gust to make precise accuracy difficult.

All this assumes, of course, fishing with floating terrestrials. Sinking terrestrials are best reserved for those times when you know that there is a certain terrestrial in the air or on the water in enough quantity that they sink in time and create underwater opportunities for fish. In reality, whether for trout (most typically), bluegills, smallmouth, crappie or some other species, running water is thought of often as best for floating terrestrials. Still water ponds and lakes are often thought best for underwater terrestrials such as a bee, ant, beetle, or similar pattern, especially when fishing for bluegills, bass, crappie, or on those cold-water northern lakes and ponds holding trout. This does not mean that they are not good for surface imitations, since ponds and lakes may border meadows and fields, which almost by definition hold a lot of ants, beetles, crickets, grasshoppers, spiders and similar land-based fish food.

Size and type of flies. There are two basic considerations in picking the size and type of terrestrial to use. The type of terrestrial might seem easy, since the best imitation would be one that matches the type of terrestrials falling—or likely to fall—into the water that you are fishing. In short, it is "matching the hatch," terrestrial style.

In some cases, there might actually be the semblance of a hatch on the water. This can happen with flying ants, when there is a heavy cicada emergence, in streams bordered by meadows filled with grasshoppers, or when a bee or wasp nest becomes disturbed. (Just make sure that you are not the one disturbing the bee, yellow jacket or wasp nest!) In these cases, you fish with what works—imitations of the terrestrial on which the fish are feeding.

In some cases, you might want to fish an imitation that is a slightly different color, size or appearance than the live terrestrial falling on the water. Often this can trigger a strike that would not come otherwise. The slight difference in color or appearance can stand out with a batch of terrestrials on the water, and sometimes provoke a strike. The same applies to a size difference, with larger, rather than smaller, often working best. Larger denotes more protein, more of a meal for the same work to a fish, thus a more attractive offering for a fish to hit.

If this fails to provoke a strike, a possible solution is to use a terrestrial that is completely different, but thrown into the same feeding lane or area where the fish have been taking off the surface. An example would be with stream trout hitting ants or beetles, but ignoring your offerings of imitations, even when cast accurately to float, drag free, in the same feeding lane.

Sometimes a different offering, such as a hopper, cricket or cicada, can take a fish, even though there might not have been any grasshoppers, crickets or cicadas on the water or in the air. It is just that the bigger morsel may attract fish when they have become complacent with usual offerings.

In pond, lake or still water conditions, the same rules apply, except without the running water. Here you can even use more of a variety of terrestrials, since there is more likelihood of a variety of terrestrials falling into the water. Realize that in these conditions, a gusty day is best, often, to blow some terrestrials into the water, even though those same gusts interfere with accurate fly casting.

Visibility of fly and use of indicators. Typically, terrestrials are tied in the color to imitate the real creature. Thus, you find ants in black, red and cinnamon; beetles in black, brown, green, bronze and similar shades; grasshoppers in green, yellow, light green, tan and brown; cicadas in white, green, and sometimes orange.

There is no reason why you cannot tie and fish a chartreuse ant, a bright red hopper, a stark white beetle or a purple cicada. In doing so, you are no longer imitating the insect color even though you might be generally imitating its shape and size. Instead, you are tying up an attractor or explorer form of a terrestrial fly. That does not mean that you will not catch fish, but it does make one wonder what in the world a self-respecting trout, bluegill, or bass thinks those bright flies just proposed actually are.

Since terrestrials are about some degree of imitation of the natural creature, natural coloration is expected. That does not preclude adding a visibility mark on any floating terrestrial. Adding such a spot of color, even though it is not visible to the fish, makes it easier to see as you work it across a still pond—the surface of which is filled with detritus or other insects—or a stream where an offering can be lost in moving glare and riffles. There are four good ways to do this, as follows:
- Bright fluorescent calf tail post on parachute flies
- Fluorescent foam post on parachute flies
- Tied or self-stick bright color foam dot
- Dot of bright fluorescent fabric paint

All of these can be accomplished while tying and can be included in any of the flies listed previously. In some cases, a particular method must be used, being dictated by the tying method itself.

For visibility, a parachute fly must necessarily use a brightly colored calf tail or colored foam post, sticking up far enough to create a visible spot of color when fished. Flies with a smooth back, such as ants, beetles, roaches and such, can use foam stick-on dots or a dot of fabric paint. With flies of different body styles in which hackles would impede visibility, it is a toss up as to how to add a spot of color. Where, for example, would you add a spot of color to a deer hair/turkey feather wing of a tiny hopper?

Admittedly, most hoppers are large enough to spot, but small size 14s could be aided with a color spot if there were a way to add one. In these and some other cases, it might be best to add a strike indicator to the leader about 18 inches up from the fly. Typically, strike indicators are used with nymphs or wet flies to indicate strikes of flies that are deep in the water column. They are seldom used with top water flies, whether that fly is a dry fly or terrestrial.

In this case, the small size of some terrestrials and the difficulty of adding a color spot to the fly can make strike indicators very useful. I do not use strike indicators to watch the strike indicator dance or disappear, but as a guide to the general area of the floating terrestrial. To use strike indicators this way, do not focus solely on the strike indicator. Focus on the general area—say a three-foot circle around the indicator—or at the far end of the leader just beyond the strike indicator. Watch for splashes, rise forms, takes, bubbles, slurps, or similar action that indicates that your fly has been taken. Naturally, you can also use strike indicators in the standard way, as an indicator of sinking terrestrials just as you would if fishing a nymph.

Casting methods, cast direction, techniques. Fishing terrestrials is not that much different in technique from fishing any fly, and the casting methods are pretty much still the same. Many terrestrials are surface patterns. Important in this as with any fishing is a drag-free float for any surface fly. On moving water or a stream or river, use an upstream or quartering upstream cast to present the fly into the feeding lane desired.

Mend the line as desired, and retrieve to prevent current from picking up a belly of line. Use a high rod to help prevent line bellying. One aid to terrestrial fishing is that most strikes are a little more vicious, a little more active, a little more positive than the gentle sups, rises, follows, and suckings that you get from dry fly fishing. This does not mean that you can be any less vigilant, only that the take and turn of the fish is often quicker and more positive than with a mayfly imitation.

As with any fishing, it often helps to try feeding lanes that are closest to you in streams first. After fishing close areas thoroughly, move to feeding lanes or currents that are a slightly longer cast.

When fishing a bank of a pond or lake from shore, often the best approach is a series of fan casts by which you start fishing almost parallel to one bank and then with a series of casts, work in a fan-like pattern to fish the entire casting range in front of you, left to right or right to left. It is a much more systematic, thorough approach than haphazardly casting around in front of you, hoping to hit the right spots—then not really being sure afterwards what areas you have hit and what you have missed.

If fishing from a boat, the same fan casting technique works well, although surface structure may dictate fishing certain areas and avoiding others that are too shallow, too muddy, too tangled or otherwise unfishable. Often shore fishing from a boat involves using an electric motor to propel forward while you and perhaps a partner make quartering casts ahead of the boat to fish selective shoreline spots as they come into casting range.

Realize that in most of this fishing, the angler in the stern is fishing "used" water. A courtesy by the bow angler in these cases is to occasionally leave an untouched area, structure or pocket for the stern angler to fish first. Switching off angling positions is also a good way to share fishing virgin water.

Dapping and dapping methods. Dapping is a method of using a long rod and shore line/leader to dabble a fly on the surface of the water. Another way to use dapping is to use a long rod and enough line on a windy day so that the fly can touch and dance on the surface with the gusts of wind.

For this, you can fish any length rod, but the longer the rod the easier the dapping, up to a point. I generally prefer fly-fishing with nine foot rods for almost all occasions, but go to a longer rod for dapping just as I switch to a shorter rod for some specialized small stream situations.

The basic technique for this, regardless of fly type, is to work close to the fish, hold the rod horizontal or at a slight upward angle with only the end of the line and leader extending from the rod tip. Use this to drop the terrestrial onto the water surface. If fishing a stream, the technique is to allow the fly to float downstream without a drag from the leader and without any visible leader or tippet on the water to possibly alert or scare fish.

If fishing on still water, often the technique is to dap the fly on the water, but periodically raise it and drop it again—almost like a terrestrial trying to escape from the water surface but falling back each time, just as it gets airborne. Naturally, this technique only works close in and is not possible when any sort of cast must be made.

If fishing a trout stream, it helps to work from behind some cover of brush, trees, or grasses, as camouflage to the art of dapping. If working still water along a lake or pond bank, trees and brush may or may not be available, but grasses along with a crouching position helps to hide you while presenting the terrestrial.

Where it is possible I like dapping particularly for grasshoppers and crickets, since these terrestrials are often struggling on the surface and as a result attract a lot of fish. By using the technique carefully, and slightly twitching the rod, dapping allows the terrestrial to move and "struggle" a little. Here the technique is to not lift the bug from the water surface, but to move it around as a struggling, kicking cricket or hopper would do. One way do this without lifting the fly from the water is to dap, and then with the other hand, hit the butt of the rod to create vibration up the rod and down the line to move and twitch the bug slightly.

Tandem terrestrial riggings. One of the neat ways to fish terrestrials and at the same time to double your chances of a hit is to fish a tandem rig. These are rigs in which there are two flies—one a floating terrestrial, the second a sinking terrestrial. Of course, you can also use a terrestrial/non-terrestrial combination, such as small popping bug/sinking bee, Chernobyl foam ant/caddis nymph, foam cicada/woolly bugger or humpy/ant as the floater/sinker, respectively. You can also use two floating or two sinking terrestrials.

Sticking to the terrestrial/terrestrial combination, you can use anything for the surface offering that floats and that will not be pulled under by the sinking terrestrial. Thus, a

McMurray ant does not work well with a weighted sinking caterpillar, but would work well with a sinking fur ant. Similarly, a floating cicada would work well with a sinking bee or McGinty pattern.

In this, you have to make some common sense decisions about what floats and whether or not it can suspend a sinking fly. For example, if you have an unweighted chenille bee, fur ant, Vernille worm, or the like, it is likely that a medium or large size foam ant, balsa McMurray ant, foam beetle, or deer hair inchworm can support the weight of these light underwater flies.

If you have a sinking terrestrial with a little lead wire wrapped on the shank, or a bead head, or small dumb bell eyes, then a more buoyant surface terrestrial is required. Something such as a foam grasshopper or foam cicada obviously works better.

Note also that in running water currents both on the top and under the surface can play a major role in how a surface or underwater fly is pulled and tugged, twisted and turned, in the current. This should not affect the floatability of those terrestrials made of foam, balsa, or other floatable, but can affect those in which the flotation is dependant upon hackle, open cell foam or similar methods and that can in time become waterlogged and sink. Underwater flies can be affected also, because they can be pulled with the current. This is not a factor in still water, other than with surface ripples and small surface waves and chop.

There are many ways to rig tandem flies, regardless of their terrestrial/non-terrestrial labeling. Three good basic ways include the following:

Use an extra long tippet (about 18 inches longer than normal) and tie it to the leader leaving an extra long (about 18 inches) tag end. Tie the surface terrestrial to the tippet with an improved clinch knot, Palomar, or similar knot. Tie the second terrestrial to the tag end of the tippet, so that you have two flies on "two" tippets extending from the leader.

Use a very long tippet section (about 18 inches longer than normal) and tie the terrestrial to the leader leaving a very long tag end of about 15–18 inches from the knot. Then tie the sinking terrestrial to the end of the tag end. Naturally, before tying you can adjust the length of the tippet extending from the surface fly to the sinking fly.

Use a regular tippet length and tie the floating terrestrial to the end using your favorite knot. Cut a length of the same or similar size (strength) tippet about 18 inches long. Tie this extra tippet section to the bend of the surface fly hook using an improved clinch knot. Then use an improved clinch knot or Palomar knot to tie the other end of this length of mono to the sinking fly. If necessary, you can adjust the strength (more or less) and, also, the length of the mono in the tandem rig extending from the surface hook bend to the eye of the sinking fly.

Fishing tandem terrestrial rigs. Basic fishing of tandem rigs starts with the cast. Too narrow a cast often causes the tippet leader end between the point fly and the dropper or tandem fly to tangle, resulting in a mess that has to be redone completely. It certainly interferes with the fishing and fishing potential and the potential of using two markedly different flies in two different parts of the water column.

For casting a tandem rig of any type, use a more open cast with a wider loop so that the line, leader, tippet and flies turn over properly, in sequence and without tangling.

Once this double rig lands on the surface with the rear tandem fly sinking, you then have to fish it.

For running water, much of your casting is most likely quartering upstream with the fly rig dancing downstream as you fish the surface and just underneath in the water column. Repeated casts to slightly different spots allows you to cover the water, using different current and feeding lanes as you fish terrestrials; if fishing straight upstream, retrieve line at the rate that matches the speed of the current. The purpose here is not to retrieve the fly faster than the current, but to maintain line retrieve at the same rate as the current speed so that you have no appreciable slack in the line when a fish hits.

Fish can hit the surface imitation, which you can see and thus then react to accordingly. Fish can also hit the underwater terrestrial, in which case you might feel the hit or just see the surface bug start to drag on the surface, almost like a strike indicator. Actually, this surface terrestrial also serves as a strike indicator, just one with a hook in it.

If fishing still water, the best approach is often a slow one. Thus, twitches and shakes of the fly rod can cause the surface bug to dance around. For this reason, I often like terrestrials with a lot of long rubber legs to get maximum life-like action to simulate a real bug. These long legs give more action to any fly when fished in running water and micro-currents and eddies or when twitched by the rod in running or still waters.

Chumming—methods and uses. Chumming in all types of fishing is a method of baiting fish with the addition of some attractant to bring them to the area where you are fishing with bait or lures. Typical chumming involves methods practiced in saltwater using ground fish, fish oil, or ground soft-shell clams, to attract striper bass and bluefish; anglers using corn broadcast to a fishing area to attract carp when still fishing; and anglers throwing terrestrials into running water to find feeding lanes and to set up fish for taking a terrestrial imitation. You can also chum terrestrials in still water, but this is a more difficult proposition with less likely results.

Before trying any chumming, make sure that it is legal where you are fishing. Some areas, states, and waterways have no rules against chumming, while in other areas it is forbidden.

The idea of chumming with terrestrials, to find and encourage trout to hit, may not have been invented by Charlie Fox and Vince Marinaro, but they certainly popularized it when developing terrestrial patterns and fishing on the LeTort in south-central Pennsylvania. Later, it was covered in various books such as *A Modern Dry Fly Code* (Marinaro, 1950). Two of the ten chapters dealt specifically with grasshoppers and Japanese beetles, and also publicized the jassid as a surface terrestrial fly.

Later, Marinaro went to even greater lengths, not so much for fishing as for studying trout, when he set up over the water edge an angled length of PVC tubing. With this, he could tumble a natural insect into a feeding lane to watch and photograph the rise forms of trout waiting at the end of the tube as the natural fell into the water.

Without the PVC tubing, you can chum as do most trout anglers, using an upstream position to toss an insect into the water, following it to see if you have the right feeding lane and then watching to see when and where a fish takes this natural. After a few times to perfect this and get the fish used to taking live insects, it is easy to switch to a casting position and drop an imitative offering where it can drift, hopefully drag-free, into the same feeding lane to be taken. And while this is a typical technique of trout fishermen on small, mostly meadow, streams in some areas, it can also be tried on any water—larger streams and rivers—and for surface-feeding smallmouth, bluegills and other panfish.

Some chumming is natural and done for you by nature or storms. An example would be after a short but violent storm in which a bank-positioned ant nest or termite mound is washed into the water to provide downstream fish with a ready and, for awhile, constant supply of surface terrestrials. Sometimes, even without a storm, a bank can give way to dump all or part of a terrestrial ant, termite or yellow jacket nest into the water.

You can also find similar possibilities during early spring when inchworms are out, suspending from their spider-like silk and occasionally dropping into the water to become fish food. The same thing can occur with some caterpillars, particularly those nasty tent caterpillars that are particularly damaging to the agricultural fruit tree business. Sometimes these can be found along streams, particularly if there are cherry or other fruit trees overhanging the water, and fall out and become fish food.

There also ways to "encourage" some of these methods of natural chumming, although the ethics and propriety of such may be subject to question by some. For example, it is entirely possible when chancing upon an ant or termite nest to stir it up, kick it or otherwise disturb it so that parts of it fall into the water. The same possibilities exist with tent caterpillars where you can use a stick to disturb a nest over the water and cause some of the caterpillars to fall into the water. Early fishing methods described killing a groundhog and hanging it from a tree limb overhanging the water so that the ensuing maggots feeding on the carcass would fall into the water to attract fish, often trout. It is automatic chumming, although the mental image of this might not be the most appealing.

In any of these cases, natural or man-made, a short but furious feeding frenzy can be triggered and create some great action and surface activity. Unlike fish that are lining up to take terrestrials from one feeding channel or lane, often this can trigger rapidly cruising fish taking any and all of the insects that they can find. As a result, accuracy in casting may be less important than getting the fly out there and into the area where fish are feeding.

While this type of chumming with individual insects or with nests is best when fishing running water, you can also take advantage of it in still water lakes and ponds, but there are differences. For example, in running water there is the possibility of finding fish feeding on terrestrials almost anywhere along a stream or river. If working with a buddy or two, you can cooperate to feed the fish (chum) insects upstream of where the fly angler is casting and try to take said fish on an imitation. The same applies to ant nests or overhanging caterpillar tents.

It is different with still water, since the lack of current prevents dispersion of the insects. Thus, you have to have two things going for you. One is the presence or strong possibility of fish being in the area to feed on the huge supply of terrestrials. The second is that you have to have insects in the area, either where you or a cooperating buddy can take turns tossing insects and catching fish, or where an overhanging tent of caterpillars or dangling inchworms drops enough insects into the water to keep the fish occupied while you figure out the right imitation and the best casting approach.

Fishing rises and rise forms. Rise forms and methods of taking vary with each fish species, but are often different with terrestrials than with other fly and patterns. Trout often delicately sip in a mayfly, although on feeding frenzies with lots of fish and lots of flies in the area, they can get into the slurping and sucking stage. Bluegills, regardless of the fly type, often make a distinct "popping" sucking sound as they take in a fly or surface bug. Smallmouth often slash at a fly, but are not against sipping in terrestrials under other conditions.

Typically, rises and takes of terrestrials are a little faster, more aggressive, slashing and slurping with smallmouth bass, panfish, and sometimes, trout. These rough-and-ready takes also occur with trout, but trout can delicately sip in a terrestrial, just as they do a mayfly. This more usually occurs with small terrestrials such as ants and small beetles than with crickets, hoppers or cicada killers, but it is not uncommon to have a delicate, inspecting rise form.

In all cases, allow the fish to turn and dive or swing away from the terrestrial and take the fly to securely set the hook. Hook setting in these cases is more allowing the fish to take the fly and move, to set the hook itself, than involving the angler doing anything. In the case of the active, moving, slashing or slurping takes, often the fish hooks itself even before diving or moving. They are so intent in feeding that they inhale the fly and are hooked solidly almost immediately.

Striking the fish. With fine tippets often used with small terrestrials, use a slip strike rather than a positive hand/rod strike. This slip strike is nothing more than moving the rod tip sideways as the fish takes to cause a little pressure—enough to set the fine hook point—into the fish. Because the line slips through the guides, it is called a slip strike and it also prevents a hard solid strike which could snap the leader tippet.

Blind casting and fishing. Since any terrestrial is an occasional meal and possible target for a fish, terrestrials are good explorer flies when fishing new water, old water under new conditions, during unusual weather conditions, or when fish are not rising or otherwise visibly noticeable. Thus, blind casting is often a good way to find fish, particularly if surface fishing or under conditions when fish might take surface offerings. Just how you do this depends upon the water being fished.

If fishing a pond, cove of a lake, or any still water, the best approach is to fan cast so that you cover all of the water. By fan casting, say from left to right around your position, you cover all the water within casting range. Make each cast so that the terrestrial lands within a few feet at most of the first cast. The reason is that most fish travel a few feet at most to explore a possible meal, but this also dictates a slow twitching retrieve that helps simulate the action of the terrestrial on the water. If fishing an ant or beetle, use a very slow retrieve, moving the fly only a few inches at a time, and then allow it to rest. If fishing a hopper, cricket, cicada killer or cicada, then move the fly farther and more rapidly as would be consistent with the movement of the live insect.

By making fan casts, you cover a large area that is equal to the angle of the fan cast range by the length of your typical cast. That angle or cast could be narrow to approach a pocket between a boat dock and lily pad bed, or on a small pool on a trout stream.

It could be larger—say 180 degrees—as when fishing for trout in a long, large open pool on a big slow river or if bass fishing a pad-specked cove on a big lake.

The previously mentioned technique basically applies to open water. In still water with structure for bass or bluegills, other conditions apply. Most bass and panfish like structure, pads and grass. The grass can vary from eel grass to pond weed to hydrilla or any other type native (or not!) to your area. Structure can include docks, piers, riprap, sunken boats, stumps, standing timber, brush piles, breaklines, log jams, rock piles, etc.

Any of these are good spots for panfish, crappie, perch and bass in particular. As a result of this fishy-looking cover, this might not be considered blind fishing, but it is in one sense if there is no visible evidence of fish life. In these situations, the best casts are not fan casts in this limited area, but casts that cover the fishy-looking cover thoroughly. Since many of the fish sought are schooling fish, the best approach is to make the first casts to the outside of what looks like the best area. If you do get a strike, it allows taking that fish out of the cover area and hopefully fighting it in open water where it cannot unduly scare other fish that are closer to the structure. This then allows making a series of casts to hook fish as you work closer to the main structure or hot spot, or at least to not scare closer fish. If you do not hook fish, then they are likely not in that area, and a cast to the prime spot is in order.

The other disadvantage to casting initially to the prime spot is that this can "line" other fish that are between you and the prime target. These lined fish can scare the entire school or other fish in that same area. As a result, an initial cast to prime targets can destroy the fishing possibilities for that entire location, making your careful approach by wading or boat movement useless.

Stream fishing is different in that you have the presence or absence of structure as above, along with the varying depths and currents of running water. In some cases, there might be no structure, but instead a back eddy of water, a change of water flow, an edge of fast and very slow currents, a waterfall creating highly oxygenated water, riffles at the tail of a pool, pocket water, or a long gravel and rock pool.

AFTERWORD

The point of fishing is to catch fish—and have fun. The point of fly-fishing is to catch fish using that most pleasurable equipment—fly-fishing gear. The point of fly-fishing gear is the challenge of catching fish on small flies that are usually tied to resemble live bait or natural fish food.

Terrestrials—even though land based—fit right into this scheme of things. They fall into the water where they end up on the menu of gamefish. While some are small and merely fish snacks (some ants and beetles) some are large (grasshoppers, crickets, inchworms, cicadas) to make for a big munchy meal for most fish. Terrestrials are fun to tie, fun to cast and fun as fish-catchers.

The bottom line with terrestrials is to keep their tying simple. Unless you wish, don't get hung up on the entomology and exact simulation of each species of terrestrial, or how each species of fish might react to it. Fish react fine to simple terrestrial patterns. Fish are opportunistic feeders, and most gulp anything that looks like a meal, and even some things that do not. Trout have been caught and when necropsied, had stomach contents that included cigarette filters, parts of tossed away plastic lures, candy wrappers, chewing gum, sticks, and foam packing peanuts. The list is endless.

Terrestrials make up a good supply of food for all manner of fish that feed on top and in the mid-depths of the water column. When tying or thinking about tying a pattern for terrestrials, think first of size, then color, followed in order by general shape, legs and any other parts that might be a visual signal for a fish and help trigger a strike.

Size is easy, since it revolves around the multitude of hook sizes available and whether regular or long shank. Color is easy, since all fly tying materials come in a rainbow of colors. General shape revolves around how you tie and what you use to tie up a fat little stink bug, a big cicada, a slim leafhopper, flattened click beetle or tiny ant.

The bottom line is that fish don't have the brain power to care which terrestrial lands on the ceiling of their lair, and are less concerned about whether it exactly matches their concept of a meal. It must match their visceral triggering mechanisms. They are going to hit it or not, depending upon hunger and whether or not it looks buggy. Fortunately, all terrestrials look buggy.

The bottom line with terrestrials is to have fun in tying them, develop your own designs (or use those in this book), enjoy fishing with them, and have fun. Innovate, explore with materials at the bench and learn from fishing techniques on the stream. Try new materials, new designs, and new ways of tying.

Have fun—that is the goal. These funny little land-based patterns can add a lot to our tying fun and fishing enjoyment, regardless of the terrestrial thrown or the species sought. Enjoy.

BIBLIOGRAPHY

Almy, Gerald. *Tying & Fishing Terrestrials*, Mechanicsburg, PA: Stackpole Books, 1978.

Bartholomew, Marty. *Tying Flies Like a Pro*, Portland, OR: Frank Amato Publications, 2006.

Engle, Ed. *Tying Small Flies*, Mechanicsburg, PA: Stackpole Books, 2004.

Fullum, Jay "Fishy." *Fishy's Favorites*, Mechanicsburg, PA: Stackpole Books, 2006.

Fullum, Jay "Fishy." *Fishy's Flies*, Mechanicsburg, PA: Stackpole Books, 2002.

Koch, Ed. *Terrestrial Fishing*, Mechanicsburg, PA: Stackpole Books, 1990.

Schmidt, William E. *Hooks for the Fly*, Mechanicsburg, PA: Stackpole Books, 119 pages. 2000.

Skilton, Bill. *My Fly Patterns, Materials and Techniques*, Boiling Spring, PA: USA-Flies, 2002.

Steeves, Harrison R, III. *Tying Flies with Foam Fur and Feathers*, Mechanicsburg, PA: Stackpole Books, 2003.

Steeves, Harrison R. III and Koch, Ed. *Terrestrials*, Mechanicsburg, PA: Stackpole Books, 1994.

Wilson, Loring D. *Tying and Fishing the Terrestrials*, Cranbury, NJ: A. S. Barnes and Co., Inc., 1978.

INDEX